What America Gave Me

Even Though I've Never Been There (Yet!)

Lu Bega

Introduction

I was born in June 1986 in Kraków, Poland, just a few months after the world was shaken—quite literally—by the Chernobyl disaster. Now, if you're an American reader who doesn't quite recall what that was (or maybe you've only heard about it through a Netflix series), let me paint a picture. Chernobyl was a nuclear power plant in what is now Ukraine, and it was the site of one of the most catastrophic accidents in human history. On April 26, 1986, reactor No. 4 exploded during a safety test. Yes, you read that right. A *safety* test. This resulted in a radioactive cloud floating over much of Europe, including my not-so-fortunate homeland.

To protect the people, or at least try to, my mother—along with many others in Poland—was forced to drink Lugol's iodine solution, which was supposed to stop the thyroid from absorbing radioactive iodine. Imagine being told that chugging some medical-grade iodine was your best bet to avoid radioactive poisoning. Good times.

But the fun didn't stop there, because this all happened in a communist state—a time when life was a peculiar mix of fear, shortages, and endless grey. And, of course, we can't forget the wonderful economic model of *central planning,* better known as the "economy of shortages." It was a system where the government planned everything… poorly. Everything from bread to toilet paper was in short supply. Imagine waiting in line for hours just to get a loaf of bread, only to find out that the guy in front of you bought the last one. Yes, that was life in communist Poland.

Now, how did Poland, a proud and ancient nation, find itself under the heel of the Soviet Union? Well, it's a bit of a long story, but it all goes back to World War II. You see, Poland was technically on the winning side of the war, but somehow still managed to get shafted in the process. At the Yalta Conference in 1945, the Western Allies—Roosevelt and Churchill—more or less handed Poland over to Stalin. It was a "thanks for your service, but we'll be taking it from here" kind of deal. So, while America and the West celebrated their victory, Poland entered a whole new era of oppression, this time courtesy of our "liberators" from the East. You have to admit, there's some dark irony there.

Communism, for the uninitiated, is a system where the state controls everything. And by everything, I mean absolutely everything—from the factories producing goods to the bread on your table (if you were lucky enough to find any). It was a system designed to ensure equality—by making sure everyone equally lacked everything. The only thing in abundance was propaganda, and let me tell you, we had some *great* propaganda.

Life under communism wasn't exactly bursting with color either. You see, grey wasn't just the color of the Soviet uniforms; it was the color of our daily lives. The buildings? Grey. The skies? Probably grey too. And the mood? Well, let's just say optimism wasn't really a big thing. It was a world of grey tones and shortages, and yet, amidst all that, something from the West still managed to creep in… America.

Growing up in communist Poland, one thing was clear: if you wanted to live the "good life," you had to leave. And many did just that—well, *escaped* might be a more accurate term. A significant number of Poles, including my relatives, packed their bags (or left them behind entirely) and fled to the West. A popular destination? The United States of America. The land of opportunity, freedom, and, most importantly, blue jeans.

The stories that filtered back to Poland from those brave (and lucky) enough to make it out painted a picture of a paradise. They spoke of streets lined with gold—or at least streets where you could find more than one kind of bread. In communist Poland, the average wage was something laughable, around 2 cents per hour, if you converted it to US dollars. Meanwhile, in the glorious land of America, newcomers were greeted with a starting wage of 6 dollars an hour. Six dollars! For a Pole stuck in the drudgery of the centrally planned economy, that was like winning the lottery—every hour.

But it wasn't just the money. It was the *stuff*. You see, in Poland, thanks to our wonderfully efficient *gospodarka niedoborów* (economy of shortages), you couldn't just walk into a store and buy what you needed. Most of the time, stores had one or two things in stock, and neither of them were what you wanted. But in America? People lived in a world where you could choose what brand of toothpaste to buy. *Multiple brands!* It was like another universe.

And then, slowly but surely, some of that Western abundance started to trickle into Poland, thanks to the ingenuity of our émigré relatives. I remember the first time I saw a pair of American jeans. They weren't just pants; they were a symbol and an icon of everything the West represented. Freedom. Choice. Style. Owning a pair of Levi's was like wearing the American Dream on your legs. And if you had a pair of Western sneakers? You were practically a celebrity.

It wasn't just clothes, either. American pop culture began to slip through the Iron Curtain, albeit in small doses. Someone's cousin would come back from America with a suitcase full of cassette tapes. Suddenly, you could listen to *real* music, not the state-approved marching anthems or the folk songs that made you want to weep. American rock bands like Metallica and AC/DC, pop icons like Michael Jackson and Madonna—these weren't just artists; they were voices from another world, a world where people had fun, where they danced and sang instead of waiting in line for toilet paper.

And don't get me started on movies. Watching an American action film, with its car chases, explosions, and unbreakable heroes, was like seeing the world in full color for the first time. Compared to the drab, state-controlled media we were used to, these films were pure magic. They showed us a life that seemed impossible: fast cars, neon lights, big houses with swimming pools. While we had grey buildings and long lines, America had *everything.*

This wasn't just consumerism. These goods and this culture were like windows to a different reality. Every pair of Levi's, every cassette tape, every bootleg VHS of *Rambo* or *Terminator* represented freedom in its most tangible form. It was proof that a better life was possible, even if it was happening on the other side of the world.

And now, dear readers, allow me to show you how the greatness of American culture influenced me, shaped my growth, and impacted my life—despite the fact that I've never stepped foot outside Europe. In fact, I can confidently say that in all of America, the only person who knew of my existence was my aunt—well, technically my mom's friend, Anna—who lived in Texas.

Yes, Texas. The land of cowboys, BBQ, and wide-open spaces. While I was stuck in the grey monotony of communist Poland, she was living her best life in the heart of the Wild West (or so it seemed to me). And although I never met her in person, her letters, stories, and the occasional care package full of Western wonders gave me a glimpse into that far-off land of freedom and prosperity.

Through her, America became more than just a distant place on the map. It became a part of my life. So, even though I've never left the European continent, America has shaped me in ways that go far beyond geography.

Cars and Motorcycles – The American Dream on Wheels

Before we dive into the roar of American muscle cars and the rumble of Harley-Davidsons, it's only fair to give you a little background on what we in Poland had to work with. Trust me, once you see the contrast, you'll understand why American cars seemed like something from another planet.

Syrena (1957–1983)

First, let's talk about Syrena. Imagine this: a car so small, so humble, yet considered a marvel of Polish engineering. The Syrena was powered by a two-stroke engine originally designed for a fire pump. Yes, you read that correctly *a fire pump*. But this was communist Poland, and in the land of shortages, why design a new engine for a car when you already had one lying around?

This little car was the first vehicle my grandparents ever owned. My grandmother still fondly recalls how my grandfather, with stars in his eyes, declared that this car would last them a lifetime. Spoiler alert: it didn't. The Syrena had all the elegance of a box on wheels, but for a generation of Poles, it was freedom. The top-of-the-line Syrena 105 could reach a blistering 80 km/h (50 mph), though it sounded like it was begging for mercy at that speed.

In contrast, in 1957, when the Syrena first hit the roads, Americans were rolling out beasts like the **Chevrolet Bel Air** with a 4.6-liter V8 engine that produced around 225 horsepower—enough to launch you down the highway like a rocket. While we were puttering along in our two-stroke miracle, Americans were cruising in style, sipping milkshakes at drive-ins, which we Poles didn't even know existed for another 40 years.

Warszawa M20 (1951–1973)

Next up, the Warszawa M20—a licensed copy of the Soviet GAZ M20 Pobeda, which was Stalin's generous gift to us instead of the more modern Fiat we had hoped for. The car itself wasn't entirely bad when it first came out; in fact, its design was inspired by American cars of the 1940s. The problem? It remained stuck in time. While American cars evolved, the Warszawa was produced for over two decades with minimal changes, becoming an outdated relic.

By the time it was rolling off the assembly lines in the 1960s, America was already pumping out the legendary **Ford Mustang** (1964), with its sleek design and powerful 4.7-liter V8 engine. The Mustang became the poster child for freedom and speed, offering 210 horsepower compared to the Warszawa's 50-60 horsepower, making the Polish car seem like a horse-drawn carriage by comparison.

Fiat 125p (1967–1991)

photo by Paul Botzenhardt

Ah, the Fiat 125p—known affectionately as the "Duży Fiat" (Big Fiat). This car was supposed to be the pride of Poland, a product of a licensing deal with Italy. But while the Italians moved on to more modern and sleek designs, we, of course, settled for the older, outdated mechanics of the Fiat 1300/1500, wrapped up in a shiny new body.

The Fiat 125p had a 1.5-liter engine producing around 75 horsepower. Not bad by Polish standards, but laughable when you compare it to the **Chevrolet Camaro** of 1967, which came equipped with a 5.7-liter V8 engine capable of producing over 300 horsepower. The Camaro could go from 0 to 60 mph in about 5.4 seconds, while the Fiat 125p... well, it just *got there eventually*.

Fiat 126p (1972–2000)

Now, the Fiat 126p or "Maluch" (The Little One) is the car that truly motorized Poland. This tiny machine had a 650cc engine producing a jaw-dropping 24 horsepower. Yes, you read that right *twenty-four* horses under the hood. It was my first car, my second car, and my fourth car. Despite its laughable power, the Maluch was a symbol of Polish resilience. Families of four (sometimes more!) would pack into this little box on wheels, loading it up with luggage, sometimes even towing trailers, and set off on epic journeys across Eastern Europe.

You could fix almost anything on the Maluch with a couple of wrenches, a screwdriver, and two hammers—no fancy tools required. Need a full engine overhaul? Just pull into your local apartment block parking lot and get to work.

By the time the Maluch hit the roads, Americans were already cruising around in the **Dodge Charger** (1966–1978), a car with an engine that could produce over 375 horsepower. The Charger was everything the Maluch wasn't - big, fast, and loud. While Polish families were squeezing into a car the size of a shoebox, Americans were living their best lives in cars that could outrun the wind.

Polonez (1978–2002)

Finally, we arrive at the Polonez, the pride of Polish engineering—or at least that's what we were told. The design came from the legendary Italian designer Giorgetto Giugiaro, but it was the design Fiat rejected. Underneath its slightly more modern exterior, it was still a Fiat 125p in disguise, with the same outdated mechanicals. It didn't help that the car had a reputation for being as slow as it looked, with a 1.5-liter engine producing a modest 75 horsepower. The Polonez gained a bit of fame (or infamy) outside of Poland, thanks to none other than Jeremy Clarkson of *Top Gear* fame. Clarkson, known for his brutal honesty, once reviewed the Polonez and, unsurprisingly, was not a fan. He described it as "one of the worst cars in the world," calling it slow, uncomfortable, and outdated even by the standards of its time.

But Clarkson didn't stop at just words. In true *Top Gear* fashion, he decided to make a statement about the Polonez's durability—or lack thereof—by hoisting one high into the air with a crane... and then dropping it. Needless to say, the Polonez did not survive the fall. The crash was a spectacular one, symbolizing, in a way, the end of an era for Polish car manufacturing. As Clarkson would put it, "If this car was made from metal, it's incredibly light. If it was made from cheese, it's incredibly strong."

While Clarkson's dramatic review of the Polonez was a bit exaggerated for entertainment, it did highlight the harsh reality: compared to the American cars of the same era, like the **Pontiac Firebird Trans Am** with its roaring 6.6-liter V8 engine, the Polonez simply couldn't compete. The Firebird was all about speed and power, while the Polonez was about... getting from A to B, eventually.

I've already mentioned that the Fiat 126p, or *Maluch*, was my first car. Actually, it was my second and fourth car too. And you know what? I believe that one day, I'll have another one sitting in my garage. The prices of *Maluchs* have shot through the roof now. I remember selling my last one for a mere 100 złotych (around $25 at the time) because I had just upgraded to a *Western* car—a Ford Escort 1.4 from the early '90s. A guy came to buy the Maluch and, of course, he haggled with me, as you do. In the end, I sold it for 80 złotych (about $20), which didn't even cover half a tank of gas in the Escort. Now? A well-preserved *Maluch* can set you back anywhere between 20,000 to 30,000 złotych (about $5,000 to $7,500). Funny how things change, isn't it?

But when it comes to legendary cars, there's one that's always been at the top of my list—*the Chevrolet Corvette C4*. With its digital dashboard and pop-up headlights, this was the car of my dreams. I used to have a poster of the C4 on my wall, and I would fall asleep staring at it, imagining the day I'd own one. And it wasn't just on the poster—I had a Turbo gum sticker of the red Corvette C4 in my pencil case. Now, if you don't know what

Turbo gum is, let me explain: it was a classic bubble gum from my childhood, and each piece came with a small card featuring a picture of a car. For Polish kids like me, it was our introduction to the world of dream machines Porsche, Ferrari, Lamborghini, and, of course, the Corvette. Chewing that gum and collecting the stickers was as close as we could get to these exotic cars. Can you imagine how would a red C4 look parked under a *trzepak* (a metal frame used for beating rugs, very popular in communist countries) in a grey communist housing estate? I'll give you a hint—it would look like it's from another world.

Another American icon - at least for me? The *Chrysler 300C* or *200C* I can't recall it now and also I'm not sure what year it was - I'm guessing - late 90's. When I was a teenager, my girlfriend's father had one—a silver beast that looked like a spaceship compared to all the *Maluchs*, *Polonezes*, and *Fiats* around. It was a symbol of pure luxury. Unlike the vinyl seats we were used to—seats that froze solid in winter and melted onto your skin in summer—the 300C had beautiful beige leather seats. The dashboard was finished with real wood, and it had air conditioning—something that had been common in American cars since the 1950s, but which I experienced for the first time in that car. I'll never forget how that Chrysler stood out. It was a glimpse of the high life.

And then, of course, there are the muscle cars that fueled my dreams. The *Plymouth RoadRunner Superbird*, with its gigantic rear spoiler, looked like something out of a cartoon but was an absolute beast on the road. And the *Dodge Charger?* Now that's the definition of a badass car. Its aggressive lines and the sound of that engine—it's pure American muscle and a car that's captivated me for years.

But how could I forget the *Ford Mustang*? Especially the *Mach 1* and the generations that followed. The Mustang is the ultimate American legend. From its sleek design to its roaring engine, the Mustang is the epitome of cool. The Mach 1, with its aggressive stance and powerful V8, was a car that stood out even among muscle cars. Whether it's the classic versions or the more modern iterations, the Mustang has always represented speed, power, and freedom. It's a car that has appeared in countless films, a symbol of American ingenuity and performance. To this day, the Mustang remains one of my greatest automotive dreams.

And speaking of dreams, let's not forget the *pony cars* and *muscle cars* that defined an era. Cars like the *Chevrolet Camaro*, the *Pontiac GTO*, and the *Dodge Challenger*—these were the beasts that roared across American highways and straight into my imagination. Pony cars like the Camaro were smaller but still packed plenty of punch, designed to be fast and affordable for the masses, while the muscle cars were all about raw power and performance. These were the machines that embodied American ambition—big, bold, and built for speed.

Even something as simple as the iconic *Ford Crown Victoria*—New York's legendary yellow taxis—seemed majestic and exotic. Seeing them in movies, with their distinct look and reliability, I thought they were some of the best cars out there. Funny how even a taxi in the States could stir up so much admiration.

Motorcycles – Two Wheels, Two Different Worlds

Poland's motorcycle industry has an interesting, albeit turbulent, history. From the impressive craftsmanship of pre-war models to the more utilitarian bikes of the communist era, Polish motorcycles reflect the challenges of their times. However, when you compare these Polish two-wheelers to the roaring giants coming out of America, the differences become as clear as night and day.

Sokół 1000 (1934–1939)

Let's start with a true Polish legend—*Sokół 1000*. Produced before World War II by the PZInż (Państwowe Zakłady Inżynierii), the Sokół 1000 was the pride of the Polish military and police forces. It was designed to be robust, reliable, and ready for rough terrains, much like the iconic American motorcycles of the time. The Sokół was equipped with a 1,000cc V-twin engine, producing around 22 horsepower, which was impressive for its era. It could reach a top speed of around 100 km/h (62 mph), which was quite respectable for the 1930s.

However, while the Sokół was a solid machine, it had to compete with the likes of the **Harley-Davidson EL Knucklehead** (1936), which was similarly equipped with a 1,000cc engine. But the Harley's V-twin could produce up to 40 horsepower, nearly double that of the Sokół. The Knucklehead was also more refined, with superior suspension and more advanced engineering. In a sense, the Sokół 1000 was Poland's answer to Harley-Davidson, but given the limited resources and the approach of war, its production was cut short in 1939.

Junak (1956–1965)

Fast forward to post-war Poland, and we have the *Junak*, produced by the Szczecin-based factory. For Poles, the Junak was the closest thing to a heavyweight motorcycle that we could dream of during the communist era. The Junak M10, introduced in the late 1950s, boasted a 350cc single-cylinder engine, which produced around 17 horsepower. It was a sturdy and relatively powerful machine for its time, with a top speed of about 110 km/h (68 mph). It was well-regarded for its reliability and rugged design, making it a popular choice for Polish motorcyclists.

Unfortunately, the Junak had no real answer to the **Harley-Davidson Hydra-Glide** (introduced in 1949 and later versions in the 1950s), which came equipped with a 1,200cc engine capable of producing over 45 horsepower. The Hydra-Glide, with its smooth ride and iconic styling, embodied everything that American motorcycles stood for—power, comfort, and style. While the Junak got the job done, the Harley was a dream machine, representing freedom on the open road.

WSK (1954–1985)

As we move into the 1960s and 70s, the Polish motorcycle scene became increasingly utilitarian. Enter *WSK* (Wytwórnia Sprzętu Komunikacyjnego - Transport Equipment Factory), a factory that produced small, simple motorcycles designed for everyday use. The WSK M06, one of the most popular models, came with a 125cc two-stroke engine, producing a modest 7 horsepower. It was a lightweight motorcycle with a top speed of around 80 km/h (50 mph), and it was affordable, making it accessible to the average Polish citizen.

Of course, many joked that WSK didn't really stand for Wytwórnia Sprzętu Komunikacyjnego, but rather *Wiejski Sprzęt Kaskaderski*—"Stunt Equipment for Villagers." And it was easy to see why: riding one on Poland's rough, unpaved roads could sometimes feel like you were performing your own stunt show.

By comparison, American riders at the time were getting their hands on bikes like the **Harley-Davidson Sportster** (1957), which came equipped with a 900cc V-twin engine, producing over 55 horsepower. The Sportster was not just a bike—it was a symbol of American independence and rebellion. It could hit speeds of over 160 km/h (100 mph), leaving the WSK far behind in both power and performance.

Panonnia (1954–1975)

One of the more unique motorcycles in the Eastern Bloc was the *Panonnia*, a Hungarian-made bike that gained popularity for its reliability and rugged design. My Grandparents owned one, a sleek black model with a striking red seat as this one in the picture. The Panonnia was more than just a motorcycle, it was a symbol of adventure and freedom for many families. With a 250cc two-stroke engine producing around 14-16 horsepower, it wasn't a speed demon, but it was dependable and perfect for getting around in rural and urban areas alike.

Compared to the more common Polish bikes, the Panonnia stood out with its larger, more robust frame, and its distinctive design. Its combination of black bodywork and the red seat gave it a bit of flair that made it memorable for me.

While it wasn't as powerful as some Western bikes, and certainly nowhere near the likes of Harley-Davidson or Indian, it had its own charm. For a time, it was the pride of Hungarian motorcycle engineering.

Today, I dream of buying a Panonnia again, so that my Grandparents can relive those moments from their youth. Time is running out, though, as my *Dziadziuś* (Grandad) is now 91 and my *Babunia* (Grandmother) is 87. It would be incredible to see them smile at the sight of that black bike with the red seat, bringing back memories of days gone by. A funny story often told by my *Babunia* is that she would repeatedly urge my *Dziadziuś*, asking if he couldn't go faster on that thing!. Now I know where my need for speed comes from! *Dziękuję Babuniu!* (Thank you Grandma!)

WFM (1951–1975)

Another staple of Polish motorcycling was *WFM* (Warszawska Fabryka Motocykli), which, like WSK, focused on producing small, practical bikes for the masses. The WFM M06, with its 125cc engine (producing 7 horsepower), was virtually identical to the WSK models, as both factories often shared parts and designs. The goal was simple: create a cheap, easy-to-maintain motorcycle that could handle Poland's rough roads.

While WFM was focused on affordability, in the United States, the **Harley-Davidson Electra Glide** (1965) was revolutionizing the touring market. The Electra Glide was the ultimate long-distance cruiser, with a 1,200cc engine producing around 60 horsepower and an electric starter—something unheard of on Polish bikes at the time. While the WFM was struggling to keep up with everyday needs, the Electra Glide was making cross-country tours a breeze.

Komar (1960–1983)

Now we come to the *Komar*, a motorcycle in the loosest sense of the word. The Komar was a tiny moped, powered by a 50cc two-stroke engine that produced an awe-inspiring 1.5 horsepower. It could reach a top speed of 45 km/h (28 mph) on a good day. The Komar was a practical vehicle, especially for students and people who just needed cheap transportation. It was slow, but reliable, and it symbolized mobility for many Poles during the lean years of communism.

In contrast, in the same era, American bikers were riding the **Indian Chief** (revived in the early 1950s), with a 1,200cc engine and about 40 horsepower. While the Chief was a symbol of American heritage and rugged individualism, the Komar was a symbol of "making do" in a country where resources were scarce. While Americans were riding iconic machines, Poles were happy just to have two wheels and an engine, no matter how small.

Motorynka (1978–1995)

And then there was the *Motorynka*, a tiny minibike that became a cult classic in Poland. The Motorynka MR-50 was powered by a 50cc engine and produced about 1.7 horsepower. Its top speed? A lightning-fast 45 km/h (28 mph). It was the dream of every Polish child in the 80s, and for many, it was their first experience with a motorized  vehicle. The simplicity of the Motorynka made it perfect for young riders, and it's still remembered fondly today by those who grew up during that era.

However, its reliability (or lack thereof) became legendary. If you managed to ride it for 10 miles without breaking down, it was considered a major success! Thanks to the Motorynka's frequent need for repairs, many young Poles got an early education in basic mechanics—whether they liked it or not. You weren't just riding; you were learning how to fix it on the side of the road.

Meanwhile, in the late 70s, Harley-Davidson was producing the **Harley-Davidson FX Super Glide** (introduced in 1971), with its 1,200cc engine producing over 60 horsepower. It was a bike designed for serious riding, and while American teenagers were dreaming of big, powerful bikes, Polish kids were happy to have the humble Motorynka, their gateway into the world of motorcycling.

While Polish two-wheelers like the Junak or WSK were reliable workhorses that got the job done, American motorcycles—*Harley-Davidson* and *Indian*—represented something else entirely: freedom, prosperity, and the pursuit of the open road. Even in communist Poland, where the Iron Curtain sought to block out Western influence, stories and images of these iconic bikes found their way through.

Harley-Davidson wasn't just a motorcycle—it was a cultural icon. Thanks to American films like *Easy Rider* (1969), the image of two men cruising the open highways on their Harley choppers became the very embodiment of rebellion and freedom. For young Poles, who were used to cramped apartments and state-controlled everything, seeing a Harley on screen was like catching a glimpse of a completely different life. It wasn't just a machine—it was a symbol of a lifestyle that celebrated independence and individualism, concepts that were scarce in the reality of communist Poland.

The same could be said for *Indian Motorcycles*, which, alongside Harley-Davidson, held a legendary status in the motorcycling world. Stories of these machines trickled down to Poland, often brought by those lucky enough to visit the West or by émigré relatives. They spoke of their powerful engines, smooth rides, and the unmatched craftsmanship that went into building these motorcycles. For a Polish motorcyclist who was used to repairing his WSK on the side of the road every few miles, the idea of a machine that could roar down an American highway for hours without breaking down was almost mythical.

The engineering behind these American motorcycles was perceived as revolutionary. With their powerful V-twin engines, Harleys like the **Harley-Davidson Electra Glide** or **Indian Chief** were seen as marvels of design. They weren't just about getting from point A to point B—they were designed for performance, comfort, and style. These bikes could hit speeds and distances that Polish riders could only dream of. While a WSK or Junak was built for practicality, Harleys and Indians were built for the *experience*—the sheer joy of the ride.

In the eyes of many Poles, these motorcycles represented the prosperity of the West. While they struggled with shortages and outdated technology, Americans seemed to live in a world of endless possibilities. Owning a Harley or an Indian wasn't just about having a bike—it was about having access to the best the world had to offer, both in terms of engineering and in terms of lifestyle. For those who had only seen these bikes in movies or heard stories, they became symbols of a better life, one filled with freedom, adventure, and the open road.

As a child, I spent my summers in Brzozów, a small town in the Podkarpacie (Subcarpathian) region, where my Grandparents live. Those summer days were some of my fondest memories, especially because of my friend who lived nearby. He had what every kid in Poland dreamed of—his own *Motorynka*, a tiny minibike that felt like the coolest thing on two wheels. But even more exciting than the Motorynka were the stories he would tell about his family in the United States.

His uncle who at this time lived in the US, as it turned out, owned a Harley-Davidson—a motorcycle that, to us, might as well have been a spaceship. He even had a Polaroid picture of his uncle sitting proudly on that chrome-covered Harley. We would stare at that little photo for ages, imagining what it would be like to see such a bike in real life. Riding the Motorynka around Brzozów, we'd pretend we were on that Harley, cruising the highways of America. In reality, seeing a Harley up close was something we barely dared to dream of, let alone riding one ourselves.

And today? Well, I'm 38 years old, with a full motorcycle license, and I've got thirteen tattoos—two of which are motorcycles, both designed in a Harley-Davidson style. I couldn't even count how many motorcycle-themed T-shirts I've owned over the years. Harley-Davidson, Orange County Choppers, West Coast Choppers—if it had a motorcycle on it, I probably had it in my closet at some point.

Right now, in my garage, I've got a *Moto Guzzi Breva 750*. Like a Harley, it's powered by an air-cooled V-twin engine, though with its cylinders mounted transversely. It's a great bike, and I love it—but it's not a Harley. Why not? Simple Harleys are expensive, even second hand ones and I'm still working my way up to it. But one day, when I can afford it, there will be a black Sportster parked in my garage. I can already picture it, with its modified engine and that unmistakable rumbling sound that I've always dreamed of.

At 38, I'm still that kid on the Motorynka, dreaming of Harleys. And I believe that one day, that dream will become a reality.

Music – The Soundtrack of a Revolution

Growing up in the grey monotony of communist Poland, rock and roll became my escape, my gateway to a world of freedom and expression. Bands like *Metallica*, *AC/DC*, and *Guns N' Roses* electrified my soul, providing a stark contrast to the lifeless state-approved anthems. Their rebellious spirit mirrored my own desire to break free from the rigid structure of communist life. But it wasn't just these legends of rock that shaped my musical journey—there were so many others that broadened my horizons and gave me a glimpse of worlds I could only dream of.

Jimi Hendrix, with his explosive guitar solos, and *The Doors*, with their psychedelic rock, opened my eyes to the limitless possibilities of sound and emotion. *Chuck Berry* and *Janis Joplin* brought raw energy and soul, while *Tina Turner* showed what pure power and passion looked like on stage. Meanwhile, the *Beach Boys*, with their sun-soaked California melodies, were the perfect contrast to the bleakness of communist Poland—singing about surfing and sunshine, while we were stuck in endless grey.

Then came the 90s—a new wave of raw, intense emotion that resonated with me deeply. Bands like *Nirvana*, with Kurt Cobain's tortured lyrics, and *Korn* with their angst-ridden sound, captured the feelings of alienation I often felt. *Limp Bizkit* and *Linkin Park* brought a blend of rap and rock that hit hard, with Chester Bennington's earlier band *Grey Daze* also becoming a key influence for me. *Marilyn Manson* challenged the norms and shook the status quo with his shocking imagery and bold statements, making him one of my all-time favorites—and in 2025, I'll finally get to see him live in Brno, Czech Republic, on Valentine's Day.

Alternative rock bands like *Foo Fighters*, *Tool, Nine Inch Nails*, and *Smashing Pumpkins* all fueled my passion for music, each offering something unique. The aggressive energy of *Rage Against the Machine* spoke to my sense of rebellion, while *Red Hot Chili Peppers* and *Aerosmith* brought a funk-infused, laid-back vibe that was hard to resist.

And then there's *Woodstock*. The original Woodstock festival in 1969, with its message of peace and love, has always been an inspiration. That spirit of freedom through music lives on in Poland's *Pol'and'Rock Festival* (formerly used to known as Przystanek Woodstock), where I try to go every year. I ride there on my motorcycle, camp out in a tent, and immerse myself in the best music. It's a Polish version of the American legend, and my love for it was born from the very rock that made Woodstock so iconic.

But there's one genre that has stuck with me all the way—*punk*. To this day, I still listen to bands like *The Offspring*, *Green Day*, and *The Bloodhound Gang*. Their fast-paced, irreverent lyrics and energetic music continue to fuel me, bringing back that same thrill I felt when I first heard them. Their sound may be simple, but the message of defiance and freedom has always resonated with me.

American music has always had something undeniably powerful about it. It's not just the beats or the melodies; it's the way it connects with emotions on a deeper level. Growing up in Poland, where everything seemed grey and restricted under communism, American music was like a burst of color and freedom that I couldn't find anywhere else. But why did it have such a profound effect on me? There are a few psychological reasons that explain it.

First, American music, especially rock, has always embodied rebellion. From the earliest days of *Chuck Berry* and *Elvis Presley* to *Guns N' Roses* and *Rage Against the Machine*, American rock has been about breaking the rules, questioning authority, and expressing frustration with the status quo. For a young boy in communist and then post-communist Poland, where freedom was a distant dream, that message resonated deeply. It wasn't just music; it was an anthem of resistance, a way to feel connected to a bigger world that was free from the controls I was living under.

Psychologically, music acts as a mirror to our emotions and experiences. It allows us to process feelings we might not fully understand yet. For me, listening to American rock bands helped me channel my frustration and desire for freedom in a positive way. The raw power of bands like *Metallica*, *AC/DC*, and *Nirvana* hit me at a time when I needed that outlet the most. They gave me a way to express what I felt but couldn't always put into words. It was almost like therapy—every riff and lyric was a release from the pressures of the world I was living in.

There's also the concept of **emotional contagion** in psychology, which refers to how we can "catch" emotions from others, even through music. American rock, with its high-energy performances and rebellious spirit, had the power to make me feel the emotions behind it. When *Kurt Cobain* sang with raw pain, or *Chester Bennington* screamed his heart out, I felt it too. It wasn't just about listening to music; it was about experiencing the same emotions those artists were feeling.

Moreover, American music often represents **individualism**, a core cultural value in the U.S. that celebrates self-expression, freedom, and personal identity. In contrast, the communist system I grew up in was about collective identity and uniformity. Hearing music that celebrated being different, being yourself, and standing out made me realize that I could carve my own path. Psychologically, this appeal to individualism was a beacon of hope—it showed me that I didn't have to conform to the society I was born into. I could define myself, my identity, and my life.

Then there's the nostalgic power of music. As I listened to *The Beach Boys* sing about sunny California or *Foo Fighters* blast out high-energy rock, I wasn't just hearing notes; I was imagining a different world—a world of freedom, sunshine, and possibility. This contrast between their lyrics about open highways and beaches and the grey reality of Poland made American music feel like a window into a better life. That created a strong psychological association between the music and a sense of escape and aspiration.

In the end, American music didn't just entertain me; it shaped me. It gave me a sense of identity, a way to process my emotions, and an unshakable belief in freedom and self-expression. Psychologically, it was the antidote to the controlled, limited life I had around me, and it's no wonder that it's stayed with me all these years.

One of the things that made American music even more special was how difficult it was to get your hands on it. During communist times, we didn't have easy access to Western music—far from it. Most of the time, the only way to hear *Metallica* or *The Doors* was if someone had a relative or friend who managed to bring back a cassette from abroad. When that happened, it was like gold. You'd quickly make copies of it, usually on a cheap, low-quality cassette, so you could listen to it at home. We'd sit for hours recording one tape onto another, sharing music among friends to make sure everyone could experience the magic of American rock.

Even after the fall of communism, music wasn't as easily available as it is today. Western albums didn't just appear overnight in Polish stores. It took time, and until then, we still relied on borrowed or copied tapes. You'd lend your favorite cassette to a friend, trusting them to give it back intact, or trade tapes to discover something new. In a way, the scarcity of music made it feel even more valuable. Every new album you got your hands on was a treasure, something to be cherished and listened to over and over.

The effort it took to get this music made it feel like you were part of something special—an underground community of people who craved freedom and expression. And that struggle for access only deepened my love for American rock, as it wasn't just music; it was a symbol of everything we longed for in Poland.

Pop Icons – Bringing Color to a Grey World

While rock music gave me an outlet for rebellion, it was the world of *pop* that brought energy, vibrancy, and fun to a place where those things were often in short supply. Pop stars like *Michael Jackson* and *Madonna* weren't just musicians—they were larger-than-life figures, representing a world of color, movement, and creativity that was so far removed from the grey reality of life in communist Poland.

Michael Jackson, the undisputed King of Pop, electrified the world with his iconic dance moves and groundbreaking music videos. Songs like *"Billie Jean"*, *"Thriller"*, and *"Smooth Criminal"* felt like they were beamed from another planet, and watching Jackson on stage or on TV was like seeing pure magic unfold. His presence was a cultural phenomenon, and even behind the Iron Curtain, we were captivated by his artistry.

And then there was *Madonna*, the Queen of Pop, who broke all the rules. Her bold fashion, unapologetic attitude, and hits like *"Like a Prayer"* and *"Vogue"* were anthems of self-expression and independence. Madonna's music and persona showed us that you could be whoever you wanted to be, no matter what anyone else thought—an idea that was radical in the context of Poland at the time.

But the influence of pop music didn't stop there. Tracks like *"The Twist"* by *Chubby Checker* brought a sense of joy and movement that was infectious. Who could resist that simple, irresistible dance move that became a worldwide craze? Then came *Santana*, with the soulful hit *"Smooth"* featuring *Rob Thomas*, blending Latin rhythms with rock in a way that made you want to dance no matter where you were.

Whitney Houston had a voice that could stop time. Every song she sang—from *"I Will Always Love You"* to *"I Wanna Dance with Somebody"*—was an emotional experience. Her music had a power that could make you feel deeply connected, even if you didn't speak the same language or live in the same world.

The late 90s and early 2000s brought even more icons who defined an era. *Timbaland* became a hitmaker, crafting beats that were unlike anything we'd heard before. Songs from artists like *Mary J. Blige*, *Dido*, and *Justin Timberlake* filled the airwaves with new sounds and new styles. These artists combined pop, R&B, and hip-hop to create music that was both innovative and universally appealing.

And of course, the world of hip-hop and rap made its way into Poland as well. *Eminem* and *Dr. Dre* turned the music scene on its head with raw, unfiltered lyrics and beats that were addictive. *Snoop Dogg*'s laid-back style and flow were a revelation, and suddenly, the West Coast sound became something we could all relate to, even halfway across the world. Hip-hop became more than just music—it was a cultural movement that resonated with people who felt misunderstood or marginalized.

The magic of American pop culture was that it wasn't just one-dimensional. It gave us music to dance to, music to cry to, and music to feel empowered by. It showed me that no matter how far away I was from that world, I could still be a part of it through the music. And it wasn't just *Michael* and *Madonna*—it was *Chubby Checker*, *Santana*, *Whitney Houston*, *Timbaland*, *Mary J. Blige*, *Dido*, *Eminem*, *Dr. Dre*, *Snoop Dogg*, and *Justin Timberlake*. They all brought something unique, and through their music, they brought the world a little closer, one song at a time.

And this is yet another aspect of how America influenced me, a boy from across the ocean, living in a town no one had heard of unless they were from Poland, a boy who has never been to America, though he really wishes he could. One day, I'll save enough money to fly to the States, buy or rent a motorcycle, and ride across the country from coast to coast.

Movies – Heroes, Explosions, and Big Dreams

If there's one area where American culture truly shines, it's the world of cinema. The American entertainment industry has always seemed larger than life, bringing us heroes, stories, and fantasies that have a way of capturing the imagination like nothing else. Growing up in a world where everything felt constrained, American movies opened the door to freedom, adventure, and dreams on a massive scale. Let's just say, if there was ever proof of cultural superiority, Hollywood provided it—and it's no wonder I've been captivated by it ever since.

American cinema is a world where even the most relatable, down-to-earth characters feel iconic, and where explosions are bigger, heroes are braver, and the possibilities are endless. From sitcoms to road-trip movies and epic tales of rebellion, American films have always been an escape, a guide, and a promise that life can be as grand as you want it to be.

The World of Sitcoms: Friends and How I Met Your Mother

There's a reason *Friends* became a cultural phenomenon. With its humor, heart, and timeless portrayal of friendship, it brought warmth into homes worldwide, including mine. Watching *Friends* was like being a part of an extended American family—one that was carefree, funny, and always there for each other. *How I Met Your Mother* followed suit, taking the same recipe and giving it a modern twist. Both shows presented an idealized vision of friendship, romance, and life in the big city, complete with iconic locations, hilarious misunderstandings, and an endless supply of laugh-out-loud moments. These shows didn't just entertain; they created a world you wanted to live in, a New York City where everything felt possible. Yep, that was my dream!

Stranger Things and the Mystery of Americana

Fast forward to recent times, and we get *Stranger Things*, a tribute to 80s American pop culture, sci-fi, and horror. This show encapsulates what makes American entertainment so captivating: its ability to mix nostalgia, suspense, and coming-of-age themes in a way that appeals to all ages. Set in a small town with eerie mysteries, government conspiracies, and a group of kids who take on forces far greater than themselves, *Stranger Things* captures the magic of classic American storytelling. It reminds us of the thrill of movies like *E.T.* and *The Goonies*, updated with an edge that keeps you glued to the screen.

American Pie – The Teen Comedy That Defined a Generation

If ever there was a movie that spoke to a teenage boy trying to navigate the confusing world of growing up, it was *American Pie*. This film, and its sequels—*American Pie 2*, *American Wedding*, and *American Reunion*—became the gold standard for coming-of-age comedies. The misadventures of Jim, Stifler, and the gang were outrageous and unapologetically bold, touching on all the awkwardness and hilarity of young adulthood. Scenes like Stifler's infamous fridge incident or the hilarious fake-out opening in *American Reunion* (where Jim's rocking crib scene tricks you into expecting something much less wholesome) made these films iconic. *American Pie* didn't just make me laugh; it gave me a connection to American culture that felt exciting and rebellious. Even though

American Pie came out in 1999, almost every year I set aside an 'American Pie day'—I sit down and watch it all over again. It makes me laugh just as much as it did the first time. I love it!

The Open Road – Adventures of Freedom and Rebellion

American cinema's love affair with the open road is legendary, and it's impossible not to get caught up in it. *Easy Rider* painted a portrait of two bikers embracing the American dream of freedom, while *Convoy* and *Smokey and the Bandit* brought the thrill of highway chases and the camaraderie of truckers facing off against the law. The open road became a place where anything could happen, where rules were meant to be broken, and where heroes could outrun their troubles and limitations.

Movies like *Vanishing Point* and *Thelma & Louise* took the American road-trip genre to a deeper level, exploring the personal journeys of characters breaking free from society's expectations. *Into the Wild* captured the spirit of leaving it all behind, searching for meaning in nature. Then there's *Death Proof*, Quentin Tarantino's tribute to American muscle cars and 70s thrillers, where speed and danger meet in a high-stakes, adrenaline-fueled ride.

The Straight Story (known in Poland as *Droga ku pojednaniu*) might seem a surprising addition, but it's a perfect example of America's knack for turning even the simplest journey into something deeply profound. It's a story about family, reconciliation, and the beauty of the American Midwest, all told through the quiet but powerful journey of a man on a tractor.

Road Comedies: Cannonball Run, Road Trip, and More

Comedy and road trips are an iconic pairing in American cinema, with films like *Cannonball Run* and *Road Trip* capturing the absurdity and excitement of cross-country adventures. The sequels like *European Road Trip* brought even more hilarious misunderstandings, proving that America's love for the road extends far beyond its own borders. These movies are packed with high-speed chases, bizarre encounters, and a sense of freedom that's both absurd and addictive. *Duel* and *The Hitcher* took road films into thriller territory, reminding us that the open road can be as dangerous as it is liberating. And in this tone, let's talk about:

Fast and Furious – The Thrill of Life Behind the Wheel

If there's any movie series that truly glorified life behind the wheel, it's *The Fast and the Furious*. The first three films in this iconic franchise weren't just action movies; they were an invitation to experience the adrenaline-pumping world of street racing, friendship, and high-speed chases. Watching *The Fast and the Furious* was like stepping into a world where speed was everything, loyalty was sacred, and the open road was a place to test the limits. It was impossible not to be captivated by the energy, the roaring engines, and the bold, unforgettable characters who lived their lives one quarter mile at a time.

The Fast and the Furious (2001) – The Birth of a Phenomenon

The original *Fast and the Furious* wasn't just a film; it was a cultural reset. When I saw it for the first time, I was instantly hooked. The story of undercover cop Brian O'Conner (Paul

Walker) infiltrating the world of illegal street racing was electric. Dominic Toretto (Vin Diesel), the fearless leader of the crew, became an icon with his cool, confident attitude and love for family and cars. The modified cars—sleek, powerful, and tuned to perfection—were unlike anything I'd seen before. This movie didn't just make racing look cool; it made it look like a lifestyle.

I remember leaving the theater after watching *The Fast and the Furious* and getting behind the wheel of my Fiat 126p, trying to emulate that same speed and boldness. Sure, my little *Maluch* wasn't exactly a Toyota Supra, but for a few moments, I felt like I was part of that world. Suddenly, everyone wanted to be like Brian and Dom. That film didn't just entertain—it created a community, inspiring car enthusiasts around the globe.

2 Fast 2 Furious (2003) – Raising the Stakes

The sequel, *2 Fast 2 Furious*, took the action and speed to a whole new level. This time, the story followed Brian as he teamed up with an old friend, Roman Pearce (Tyrese Gibson), in Miami. The sun-drenched streets of Florida and the glamorous vibe of the Miami car scene made the film feel like a celebration of speed and style. From drag races to death-defying stunts, *2 Fast 2 Furious* showed a world where every race was a thrill, and the stakes were higher than ever.

The chemistry between Brian and Roman added a fun, comedic edge, but it was the cars that stole the show once again. Brightly colored, customized to perfection, each vehicle was a character in itself. This film cemented the *Fast and Furious* brand as more than just a racing movie—it was now a lifestyle, a dream of living life on the edge with the sun on your back and the engine roaring beneath you.

The Fast and the Furious: Tokyo Drift (2006) – A New Chapter in the Fast Life

With *Tokyo Drift*, the franchise shifted gears, introducing audiences to the art of drifting in the heart of Tokyo's underground racing scene. This third installment was a fresh take on the world of high-speed racing, taking the action to a whole new cultural landscape. *Tokyo Drift* was all about precision, skill, and the elegance of drifting around tight corners at impossible speeds. Sean Boswell (Lucas Black), a newcomer to the scene, had to learn the ropes from scratch, discovering that racing wasn't just about raw speed but control and technique.

The Japanese car culture brought a new visual style to the series, with cars that were sleek, futuristic, and flawlessly tuned for drifting. The neon-lit streets, vibrant night scenes, and breathtaking car maneuvers made Tokyo feel like a character itself. Watching *Tokyo Drift* introduced me—and countless others—to a whole new level of appreciation for the artistry and skill behind drifting. It wasn't just about winning; it was about mastering the craft and making every turn look like a dance.

The Legacy of Fast and Furious – Everyone Wanted to Be Brian and Dom

These first three *Fast and Furious* films captured something incredible: they turned driving into a passion, a way of life that felt both dangerous and exciting. They made every viewer feel that with the right car and the right mindset, they could be part of something bigger. After the first movie, I found myself pushing my Fiat 126p to its limits, imagining for a moment that I was in one of those turbocharged beasts from the movie. And I wasn't alone—everybody wanted to be like Brian and Dom. *Fast and Furious* didn't just create memorable films; it created an entire culture around cars, speed, and the thrill of the open road.

American Action Films – A Vision of Adventure and Endless Possibilities

If there's one genre that embodies America's larger-than-life attitude, it's the action film. Movies like *Rambo*, *Die Hard*, and *Terminator* were more than just high-octane thrill rides; they were windows into a world of endless possibilities and adventure, where heroes stood tall against impossible odds. Watching these movies as a kid, I saw America as a land where courage and determination could overcome any challenge—a place where, no matter how tough things got, there was always a way to win.

Rambo was a revelation. Here was a man who could survive in any environment, a one-man army taking on entire forces with nothing but his sheer will and survival skills. To me, *Rambo* wasn't just a character; he was a symbol of resilience and independence. In every explosion and every battle scene, I saw a world where people didn't back down, where strength and bravery were the keys to freedom. It was pure adrenaline, and every time I watched it, I felt like I could take on the world.

Then there was *Die Hard*. Bruce Willis's John McClane was the everyman turned hero, an ordinary cop who found himself in extraordinary circumstances. He didn't have superpowers or advanced training; he was just a regular guy who refused to give up. Watching McClane fight his way through the Nakatomi Plaza, outsmarting terrorists and surviving against all odds, made me feel that America was a place where anyone could become a hero. The way McClane mixed humor, grit, and sheer determination turned him into an icon. *Die Hard* wasn't just an action movie; it was a testament to the American spirit of never backing down.

And then came *Terminator*, with its relentless pace, futuristic themes, and Schwarzenegger's unforgettable performance. Here was a movie that wasn't just about action but about the struggle between man and machine, the battle for the future of humanity. The world of *Terminator* showed a land of incredible technology and innovation but also warned of the dangers that came with it. This mix of excitement and caution painted a picture of America as both the land of opportunity and the frontier of uncharted territory—a place where humanity constantly pushes the boundaries but must also be careful not to lose itself along the way.

These films weren't just entertainment; they shaped my vision of America as a place where anything was possible. Through their heroes, explosions, and larger-than-life stakes, they taught me that bravery and perseverance were universal values. They inspired me to believe that no obstacle was too great and that, with the right mindset, anyone could be a hero. Watching these films made me feel that America was more than just a country—it was an adventure waiting to happen.

Hollywood Magic – Dreaming Bigger with Glitz, Glamour, and Special Effects

Hollywood has always been more than just a film industry—it's a world of its own, a land of glitz, glamour, and stories that seem larger than life. Watching American movies as a kid, I felt like I was seeing a universe that operated on a different level, where everything sparkled a little brighter and the possibilities were endless. Hollywood magic had a way of making you dream bigger, convincing you that life could be as thrilling, as beautiful, and as boundless as the silver screen.

What captivated me first were the *special effects*, the explosions that lit up the night sky, the spaceships that soared through galaxies, and the dinosaurs that came roaring back to life in *Jurassic Park*. American movies had a way of making the impossible feel real, like you could reach out and touch it. For a kid growing up far from the lights of Hollywood, this glimpse into a world of cutting-edge technology and breathtaking visuals was awe-inspiring. It made me feel that nothing was out of reach and that, with the right vision, anything could be brought to life.

And then there were the *characters*. From fearless heroes to mysterious anti-heroes, these weren't just people on a screen; they were legends. Characters like Indiana Jones, Tony Stark, and Ellen Ripley felt like larger-than-life figures who defied limitations, inspiring you to think, "If they can do it, so can I." They had charisma, grit, and courage, embodying the spirit of adventure and resilience that seemed to be woven into the fabric of American storytelling. Hollywood showed me that characters could be complex, flawed, yet undeniably powerful.

Hollywood didn't just tell stories; it created entire worlds. Each movie had its own universe, filled with dreams, challenges, and ideals that made you feel like you were part of something grander. It wasn't just the movies themselves but the *spectacle* of Hollywood—the red carpets, the glamorous premieres, the iconic Hollywood sign—that created an aura of magic. This was a place where dreams were born, where anyone could become a star, and where the world came to see something extraordinary.

In a world that often felt limited, Hollywood made me feel that there was so much more out there. It taught me to dream bigger, to believe that life could be as thrilling, as unpredictable, and as filled with magic as the movies. Hollywood's stories may have been scripted, but the hope and inspiration they left behind were as real as it gets.

Escapism at Its Finest – Movies as a Window to American Freedom and Heroism

Growing up in Poland, where life often felt limited and gray, American movies were a lifeline to another world. They were more than just entertainment; they were a chance to escape, to immerse myself in a reality where everything was possible, and heroes always found a way. Through these films, I experienced freedom, adventure, and the thrill of possibility—all things that felt worlds away from my everyday life.

American movies portrayed a land where people could be whoever they wanted to be. They showed characters who had the courage to stand up for what they believed in, who defied the odds, and who always fought for freedom and justice. This wasn't the cautious, routine-driven life I knew; it was bold, unpredictable, and unapologetically free. Watching these films, I felt connected to a place where limits didn't exist, where heroes like Rocky, Indiana Jones, and John McClane took on impossible challenges and made it through with grit and determination. It was a vision of American freedom that inspired me, a reminder that there was more to life than what I saw around me.

In a world where personal freedom was often restricted, American films were an invitation to dream bigger, to imagine myself in those thrilling situations where courage and determination could change everything. These movies showed me that heroism wasn't just about superpowers or unbreakable strength—it was about the will to stand up and fight for something greater than yourself.

Each film was a temporary escape, a few hours of living in a place where anything could happen, and anyone could be a hero. They gave me hope, filling me with a sense of excitement and possibility that made the world feel just a little brighter. Through American movies, I discovered that there was a world out there full of freedom, adventure, and heroism—and even if it was just on a screen, it was real enough to inspire me every single day.

The Never-Ending List of American Hits

And this list barely scratches the surface. The American film industry has delivered so many unforgettable hits that it's impossible to remember them all. Each movie, from thrillers and action flicks to heartwarming dramas and laugh-out-loud comedies, is a testament to America's unmatched creativity and its ability to make us dream, laugh, and cry. Hollywood has given us heroes and stories that will live on forever, proving time and again why American movies are the best in the world.

TV Shows – The Window to the American Dream

I've already shared a few words about my favorite sitcoms, but now it's time to dive deeper into the world of American TV, where action, adventure, and excitement were just as captivating. American TV shows weren't just series—they were a window into a life that felt faster, brighter, and more thrilling than anything I had known. Shows like *Knight Rider*, *The A-Team*, and *Miami Vice* transported me to a world where heroes fought for justice, every chase was high-stakes, and each episode left you wanting more.

Knight Rider – The Car, the Hero, the Legend

Knight Rider wasn't just a show; it was a phenomenon. Michael Knight and his talking car, KITT, were the ultimate symbols of American cool. The futuristic, bulletproof Pontiac Trans Am seemed like something out of a dream, equipped with gadgets and AI that made it a character of its own. In Poland, where cars were functional but far from thrilling, KITT felt like magic on wheels. Watching *Knight Rider* made American life seem filled with cutting-edge technology, limitless possibilities, and a sense of adventure that was irresistible. Michael Knight wasn't just a hero—he was a lone wolf fighting for justice, and he made it look easy.

The A-Team – Heroes with Attitude

Then came *The A-Team*, a show that took teamwork, rebellion, and sheer ingenuity to new heights. Each member of the team had a distinct personality, from Hannibal's strategic genius to B.A. Baracus's brute strength and iconic mohawk. Watching *The A-Team* wasn't just about the action sequences; it was about the camaraderie, the humor, and the way they outsmarted the bad guys with clever plans and DIY inventions. The A-Team was the ultimate misfit squad, proving that you didn't need to be a traditional hero to make a difference. For a young boy watching from afar, it was a taste of American boldness and confidence—qualities that felt revolutionary.

Miami Vice – Style, Speed, and Danger

And of course, there was *Miami Vice*. Set against the neon-lit streets of Miami, this show wasn't just about the crime—it was about the lifestyle. Sonny Crockett and Ricardo Tubbs were the epitome of American cool, cruising around in sports cars, wearing designer suits, and tackling the criminal underworld with unflinching style. Miami itself became a character, with its sunny beaches, palm trees, and nightlife creating a dazzling backdrop that made every episode feel like an escape to paradise. *Miami Vice* wasn't just a show about fighting crime; it was a world of luxury, thrill, and danger that made American life seem glamorous and exciting beyond belief.

MacGyver – Ingenious Solutions

MacGyver was a hero unlike any other—a man who could turn a paperclip and a rubber band into a life-saving tool. His resourcefulness and ability to think on his feet showed a different kind of American heroism: one based on intelligence, creativity, and quick thinking. Watching *MacGyver* gave me a sense that any problem could be solved, no matter how impossible it seemed.

Breaking Bad – The Dark Side of the American Dream

Breaking Bad took the American Dream and flipped it on its head, showing a man's descent into darkness in pursuit of power and survival. Walter White's transformation from mild-mannered chemistry teacher to ruthless drug lord made us question the cost of ambition. *Breaking Bad* was gritty, intense, and gripping—a reminder that the path to success in America could sometimes take a darker turn.

The Office – Humor in the Mundane

If there was ever a show that celebrated the ordinary while making it extraordinary, it was *The Office*. With its quirky characters, awkward humor, and relatable setting, *The Office* made us laugh at the absurdities of everyday work life. Watching it felt like a slice of real American life, filled with eccentric coworkers, ridiculous situations, and surprising moments of heartfelt connection.

Twin Peaks – Mysteries of a Small Town

Twin Peaks brought a surreal edge to American television with its mix of mystery, drama, and the supernatural. David Lynch's portrayal of a small town filled with secrets and dark mysteries captivated audiences around the world. Watching *Twin Peaks* felt like peeling back the layers of an American town, revealing the strange and the eerie lurking just beneath the surface.

The X-Files – Trust No One

The X-Files was a phenomenon that turned skepticism and the paranormal into an art form. FBI agents Mulder and Scully's pursuit of truth in a world filled with conspiracies, aliens, and strange phenomena opened up a world of possibilities. Every episode was a question of belief versus logic, and it showed that in America, there were still mysteries left to explore. *The X-Files* made me believe that the world was far bigger and stranger than it seemed.

Californication – The Wild Life of the American Dreamer

Californication was like a love letter to California and the idea of the American artist. Following the wild, self-destructive life of Hank Moody, it painted a picture of the artistic side of America—one filled with rebellion, indulgence, and the quest for meaning. Hank's unapologetic lifestyle was an ode to the freedom and complexity of life on the West Coast, a reminder that America wasn't just about rules but also about breaking them.

The Big Bang Theory – Celebrating the Oddball

With *The Big Bang Theory*, American television proved that even the quirkiest, most socially awkward characters could be heroes. The show's mix of science, humor, and heart made it a hit worldwide, celebrating intelligence and friendship in a way that felt fresh. It gave a voice to the nerds, the dreamers, and everyone who dared to be different.

Dr. House – The Flawed Genius

Dr. House was a character like no other: a brilliant but deeply flawed doctor who solved medical mysteries with wit, intellect, and a healthy dose of cynicism. His brutal honesty and unconventional methods made him a symbol of the American anti-hero, someone who broke rules and questioned authority, all in pursuit of truth. Watching House showed me that even the imperfect could be heroes.

Sons of Anarchy – Brotherhood and Rebellion

Sons of Anarchy took the allure of motorcycles, rebellion, and loyalty and wove them into a dark, powerful story. This show wasn't just about action; it was about family, honor, and the hard choices that come with living outside society's boundaries. Watching it felt like being part of a rebellious, loyal brotherhood that stood up for its own, no matter the cost.

Brooklyn 9-9 – A Fresh Take on Crime-Fighting

Brooklyn 9-9 brought a unique blend of humor and crime-solving to the screen, following a squad of quirky detectives in New York. With its sharp wit and diverse cast, the show was a reminder that even serious jobs could be done with a lighthearted touch. It painted a picture of camaraderie and teamwork in a fun, relatable way.

Reacher – The Lone Hero

Reacher revived the classic lone-hero archetype. Jack Reacher's journey was filled with grit, justice, and strength—a relentless character who fought for the innocent with intelligence and brute force. Watching *Reacher* was a reminder of the classic American vigilante who lives by his own rules but still embodies a sense of honor.

Scrubs – Life, Death, and Humor

Scrubs was a heartfelt and humorous take on life in a hospital, mixing comedy with moments of true emotion. The show explored the ups and downs of being a young doctor, blending laughter with lessons about life, death, and friendship. It made medicine feel both serious and human, adding warmth to the world of American television.

Baywatch – The Allure of the American Beach

Baywatch wasn't just a TV show; it was an experience. Set on the sunny beaches of California, this iconic series brought a whole new level of excitement to television screens around the world. For a young viewer like me, watching *Baywatch* wasn't just about the lifeguard rescues or dramatic storylines—it was about the incredible allure of the actors, especially the actresses, who seemed to embody the ideal of California beauty.

Actresses like *Pamela Anderson* and *Yasmine Bleeth* made every episode a captivating experience. Their iconic slow-motion runs down the beach, sun-kissed skin, and effortless charm turned *Baywatch* into more than just a rescue show. It was sexy, glamorous, and larger than life. The bikinis, the sun, and the waves created a sense of freedom and confidence that was unlike anything I'd seen. In a way, it felt like the ultimate American dream—a life of endless summer, beauty, and adventure.

Baywatch made California's beaches look like a paradise, where every day was full of excitement and every lifeguard looked like they had just stepped off the cover of a magazine. For a boy watching from Poland, where the closest thing to such scenes was a swim at a local lake, *Baywatch* was the ultimate escape into a world of beauty, adventure, and yes—unforgettable, sexy lifeguards.

The American Suburbs and Lifestyle – A Dream of Big Houses, Manicured Lawns, and Endless Comfort

If there's one image that American TV shows have engraved in my mind, it's the picturesque American suburb—a world of wide streets, perfect lawns, and spacious homes with big front porches. Growing up watching sitcoms and dramas set in these idyllic neighborhoods, I couldn't help but marvel at the lifestyle they portrayed. Every house looked like a mansion, complete with multiple bedrooms, family rooms, and, of course, a sprawling backyard where kids could play, families could barbecue, and friends could gather for endless summer parties.

In Poland, life was different. Apartments were compact, practical, and rarely had the extra space to stretch out and relax. Seeing characters in shows like *Friends* or *How I Met Your Mother*, even *Desperate Housewives* or *The Fresh Prince of Bel-Air*, made me wonder what it would be like to grow up with that sense of spaciousness, comfort, and abundance that seemed to define American suburbia. The lifestyle portrayed wasn't just about the houses—it was about the lifestyle, the freedom, and the idea of "having it all."

The Iconic American Lawn

Every American home seemed to have an expansive, perfectly green lawn that was just as much a part of the house as any room inside. It wasn't just grass; it was a symbol. The neatly trimmed, lush lawn was a sign of pride and community, a small slice of nature that was yours to maintain and enjoy. The lawn was where kids would play catch, where dads would fire up the grill, and where families would set up folding chairs to watch the 4th of July fireworks. For me, this image was enchanting. It felt like every home was an oasis, a private paradise tucked away from the chaos of the outside world. In Poland, this idea of personal green space was a rarity, making American lawns feel like an emblem of freedom and abundance.

Big Houses, Endless Space

Then there were the houses themselves—beautiful two-story homes with large windows, garages, and sometimes even white picket fences. Each room seemed to be filled with light and had space for everyone, with kitchens big enough for the entire family and basements or attics for storage and secret projects. Even the classic American family room was a revelation—a place where families gathered to watch TV, eat snacks, and talk about their day.

In American shows, houses felt like their own worlds. Kids had their own rooms with plenty of space to express themselves, decorate, and keep their belongings. Parents had cozy bedrooms with large, comfortable beds, and often an en-suite bathroom—a level of luxury I could only dream of. There were usually separate dining rooms, living rooms, and spaces just for entertaining guests. Watching these shows, I marveled at how much space and privacy seemed to be built into American homes, and it left me imagining what it would be like to live in a place that felt so open, private, and personal all at once.

The Freedom of the Suburbs

Beyond the physical spaces, American suburbia itself felt like a magical realm. Each street looked like it had been designed for family life—calm, safe, and lined with trees. Kids rode their bikes down the streets, friends met up for games, and neighbors waved as they passed each other, creating a sense of close-knit community. For someone on the outside looking in, it was the ultimate expression of freedom and safety, a place where everyone knew each other and looked out for one another.

The suburbs felt alive with tradition. Halloween trick-or-treating, Christmas light displays, neighborhood barbecues in the summer—these events were symbols of a life filled with joy and celebration. It made me wonder what it would be like to grow up with these traditions as a part of everyday life, to experience the security of a community where families could leave their doors unlocked and kids could roam freely. It seemed like a world designed to make everyone feel welcome, where life was simpler, slower, and happier.

An Aspirational Lifestyle

In the American TV shows I watched, this suburban lifestyle was often presented as an attainable goal, something within reach for the characters. It wasn't just a fantasy but a part of the American Dream—something to work toward, cherish, and pass on to future generations. The shows gave me the sense that in America, a beautiful home in the suburbs was more than just a place to live; it was a way of life. It was about having a place to build memories, raise a family, and enjoy the little moments that make life special.

For me, watching these shows was a window into an existence that seemed perfect, with every detail—from the manicured lawns to the spacious houses and friendly neighbors—crafted to create the ideal life. It left me dreaming of one day stepping into that world, of what it might be like to walk into my own two-story house with a sprawling lawn, to wave to neighbors as I came home, and to be part of a community that felt more like an extended family.

American TV may have glamorized the suburbs, but it also sparked something in me—a desire for comfort, security, and the boundless possibilities that only seemed to exist in those dreamy, tree-lined streets. The image of American suburbia has stayed with me as the epitome of freedom, family, and happiness. For a young viewer in Poland, that world was something to admire, aspire to, and hope for.

Laugh Tracks and Heroes – A New Kind of Entertainment

American TV didn't just introduce me to a world of action and drama—it opened up a universe of humor and laughter that was refreshingly new. For a kid growing up in Poland, where television leaned toward the serious and realistic, American sitcoms were an exciting revelation. They weren't just about everyday life; they were about finding the humor in it, celebrating the oddball characters and situations that made each show memorable. The laugh tracks, colorful sets, and quirky characters created a style of entertainment that was as vibrant as it was uplifting, filled with a sense of optimism and possibility that made American comedy feel larger than life.

Sitcoms and the Art of Everyday Humor

Sitcoms like *Friends* and *How I Met Your Mother* offered a glimpse into a kind of life that was both relatable and aspirational. These shows didn't just tell jokes; they created a world where friends felt like family, where every day held new and hilarious challenges, and where even the smallest moments had a way of turning into unforgettable stories. Watching *Friends* was like being invited into the lives of Monica, Rachel, Ross, and the gang, and it made me feel that friendship was something truly magical—a bond that could make you laugh even on your hardest days. *How I Met Your Mother* took this formula and modernized it, showing us the ups and downs of love and life in the big city with its unique brand of humor and heart.

But beyond the laughter, these shows created worlds that felt open, supportive, and, most of all, fun. They made me want to be a part of that kind of life, where friends gathered at the same café or bar, sharing their highs and lows with humor, sarcasm, and a whole lot of love. American sitcoms were an invitation to laugh at the absurdity of life, to find joy in the small things, and to never take things too seriously. They were a masterclass in turning ordinary situations into extraordinary moments, with each episode leaving me feeling a little lighter, as if I'd just spent half an hour with friends.

The Power of Comedy in American Heroes

But American TV didn't just leave it at laughs; it created heroes who were funny, complex, and deeply human. Shows like *The Office*, *Scrubs*, and *Brooklyn 9-9* blended humor with heartfelt stories, creating characters who were as heroic as they were relatable. *The Office* took something as mundane as office life and turned it into a comedy classic, showing us that even in the most ordinary settings, humor and camaraderie could flourish. Michael Scott, with his awkward antics and lovable quirks, wasn't a typical hero—he was a reminder that you didn't have to be perfect to be loved.

Scrubs showed a side of American heroism that was often overlooked—the everyday courage of doctors, nurses, and hospital staff. Through humor and genuine moments of emotion, it depicted the real struggles of young doctors facing life, death, and friendship, all while using laughter as a coping mechanism. The characters of *Scrubs* were heroes not because they were extraordinary, but because they faced the everyday challenges of life with humor, heart, and resilience. Watching *Scrubs* reminded me that laughter could be a powerful tool in handling the toughest situations, a way to stay grounded even when things got difficult.

Brooklyn 9-9, on the other hand, reinvented the cop show by mixing action with humor, giving us detectives who fought crime but never took themselves too seriously. Jake Peralta and the team at the 99th Precinct showed that heroes didn't have to be grim or brooding—they could be funny, quirky, and still get the job done. The humor in *Brooklyn 9-9* didn't just entertain; it brought a sense of warmth and lightness to the serious world of law enforcement, making these characters feel like real people, not just figures on a screen.

A New, Vibrant Style of Entertainment

American TV had a way of blending humor with other genres, creating a vibrant, multi-dimensional style that was captivating. Shows like *The Big Bang Theory* introduced nerdy humor in a way that celebrated intelligence, making characters like Sheldon and Leonard not only relatable but iconic. *The Big Bang Theory* showed that you didn't have to fit in to be appreciated—being different could be celebrated, and friendships could form in the most unlikely places. This was a show that turned social misfits into beloved characters, proving that American TV had an inclusive, open-minded way of presenting people from all walks of life.

The X-Files*, a sci-fi thriller that became a cultural phenomenon, wasn't just about alien conspiracies and mysteries. It was about the partnership between Mulder and Scully, the tension and chemistry between two people who couldn't be more different. Their witty exchanges and dry humor gave the show a unique charm, making the intense storylines feel approachable. Through Mulder and Scully, *The X-Files* taught me that humor could exist even in the darkest stories, that laughter and mystery could go hand in hand.

American Comedy – A Celebration of Life

Ultimately, American comedy introduced me to a world where laughter was a part of life, where humor could be found in every situation, and where heroes didn't have to be perfect or powerful—they just had to be human. The laugh tracks, the catchphrases, the iconic lines—all of it created a kind of entertainment that felt alive, as if it were reaching out through the screen to pull me into its world. It was about celebrating life's little quirks, its ups and downs, and its endless surprises with a smile.

American TV didn't just make me laugh; it gave me a new perspective. It taught me that humor could be a form of resilience, a way to cope with challenges and connect with others. It made everyday heroes out of ordinary people, reminding me that there was something heroic in simply showing up, finding the humor, and moving forward. And in that sense, American TV became more than just entertainment; it became a reminder that life, no matter how tough, was always worth a laugh.

Fashion and Style – Dressing the American Dream

Growing up in Poland, fashion wasn't just about clothes—it was about making a statement, and American style was the ultimate statement of freedom and confidence. From Levi's jeans to classic leather jackets, Western fashion was like a badge of honor. Owning even one piece of American clothing felt like you were carrying a piece of the American dream. Every brand, every logo, every thread represented something bigger, something bold, something that wasn't easily accessible behind the Iron Curtain.

Levi's – The Jeans That Defined Freedom

If there was ever a symbol of American fashion, it was Levi's jeans. In Poland, jeans were rare and highly coveted. They weren't just pants; they were a symbol of Western freedom and individuality. While most people around me wore basic trousers that were practical and plain, Levi's offered something entirely different. The fit, the feel, the style—it was like stepping into a different world when you put on a pair of Levi's. The sturdy denim, the iconic red tab, and the copper rivets were details that spoke volumes. Levi's didn't just make you look good; they made you feel like you were part of something larger.

Owning a pair of Levi's was like joining a global club of rebels, dreamers, and explorers. In the West, people might have taken them for granted, but in Poland, they were a treasure. People went to incredible lengths to get their hands on them, with friends and relatives smuggling them in from abroad. The thrill of finally owning a pair, of slipping them on and feeling that durable, perfectly worn-in denim, was like a small taste of American life. Every time I wore

Levi's, I felt a connection to the icons of American culture who had worn them before—rock stars, movie stars, and freedom-loving individuals who embodied the spirit of the open road.

Wrangler – The Spirit of the American West

Alongside Levi's, Wrangler jeans carried a mystique of their own. Wrangler was a brand steeped in the ruggedness of the American West, of cowboys, wide-open landscapes, and endless skies. For me, Wranglers weren't just jeans; they were a taste of a life filled with adventure, grit, and resilience. The strong denim, the high-quality stitching, and that unmistakable "W" on the back pockets made Wrangler jeans feel iconic. They were tough, durable, and ready for anything—a perfect match for anyone who dreamed of living life on their terms.

When I wore Wrangler jeans, I felt like I was stepping into the boots of American cowboys, those legends of the West who embodied independence and courage. These jeans were designed to withstand rough terrain, long rides, and hard work, and that practicality made them even more desirable. In Poland, where clothing was often practical but rarely stylish, Wrangler jeans were both. They symbolized strength and endurance, qualities that made them ideal for anyone who wanted to stand out.

The Leather Jacket – A Symbol of Rebellion and Coolness

The leather jacket might be the most iconic piece of American outerwear, a garment that instantly brought to mind images of rebels, rock stars, and bikers. In American movies, leather jackets were worn by characters who lived on the edge—people who followed their own rules and didn't care what society thought. For me, the leather jacket became the ultimate symbol of American cool, a piece of clothing that could transform anyone into a hero, a renegade, or a legend.

Getting my hands on a leather jacket was a dream. It wasn't easy to find, and if you did manage to find one, it was far from affordable. But that only added to its allure. A leather jacket was more than just a piece of clothing—it was an identity, a declaration of independence. Wearing one made you feel powerful, like you could take on the world. It had the weight and feel of something permanent, something that would last, a reminder that even though fashion came and went, some styles were eternal.

In Poland, people noticed when someone wore a leather jacket. It wasn't something you saw every day, and it definitely wasn't something that went unnoticed. It carried an aura of mystery, a hint of danger, and a lot of respect. When I wore mine, I felt like I was channeling all the American icons who had made leather jackets legendary: James Dean, Marlon Brando, and all the Hollywood heroes who had worn them with an effortless, defiant confidence.

The American Influence on Polish Fashion

In a place where clothes were often functional and limited in style, American brands like Levi's and Wrangler brought a touch of glamour, freedom, and individuality. American fashion didn't just introduce us to new styles; it introduced us to a new way of thinking. It taught us that clothes could be more than just fabric—they could be an extension of who you were, a way to express your personality, dreams, and aspirations. In a world that often felt constrained, American fashion was a breath of fresh air, a reminder that style could be a form of self-expression.

And American brands didn't stop at jeans and leather jackets. From Converse sneakers to Ray-Ban sunglasses, American style offered a complete lifestyle that people around the world wanted to emulate. These brands were more than just labels; they were symbols of freedom, quality, and a way of life that felt uniquely American. They represented a country that celebrated individualism, creativity, and the power to shape your own identity.

Dressing the American Dream

Every time I wore Levi's, Wranglers, or my leather jacket, I felt like I was part of a story that was bigger than myself—a story about freedom, self-expression, and the belief that you could be whoever you wanted to be. American fashion was a way to feel connected to that dream, to believe that even if I was thousands of miles away, I could carry a piece of that spirit with me. Each stitch, each seam, each detail felt like a reminder that there was a bigger world out there, one filled with opportunity and adventure.

American fashion didn't just change the way I dressed; it changed the way I saw myself. It gave me the confidence to stand out, to embrace my individuality, and to dream big. In a world that often felt grey and uniform, American style was a splash of color, a burst of life, and a promise of something greater. It was more than just clothes—it was the American dream, woven into every thread.

Sneakers and Status Symbols – Expressing Individuality in a World of Uniformity

In a world where fashion options were limited, and uniformity was the norm, sneakers and jackets became powerful symbols of individuality. American sneakers, in particular, were like a breath of fresh air in Poland, where practical, durable footwear was the priority. Brands like Converse, Nike, and Adidas (once they became accessible) brought something more than just shoes—they brought a chance to express yourself, to stand out, to be unique in a sea of sameness. Wearing these brands was like making a silent declaration of independence, a small rebellion against a world that often felt constrained.

The Power of Sneakers – From Practical to Iconic

Sneakers were more than just shoes—they were status symbols, style statements, and a touch of the West. When brands like *Converse* and *Nike* finally made their way into Poland, they quickly became symbols of something much bigger than footwear. These weren't just comfortable shoes; they were badges of honor, each pair representing the allure of American style. Owning a pair of high-tops or brightly colored sneakers made you part of an exclusive club. They gave you confidence, made you feel like you belonged to something larger, something bold and innovative.

Converse All Stars, with their classic design, were a hit among the young, symbolizing freedom and a laid-back attitude. They became a staple of youth culture, an instant marker of Western influence. And then came *Nike*, with its athletic appeal and sleek design, making every wearer feel like they could step onto a basketball court or run alongside American icons. Each pair of Nikes brought a sense of aspiration—whether or not you played sports, you could look like a pro.

In a society where most footwear was simple and functional, these sneakers offered something far more valuable: the chance to stand out. They were something you wore with pride, knowing that you were expressing yourself in a way that felt distinctly American.

Jackets – More Than Just Outerwear

While sneakers were status symbols on your feet, American-style jackets were statements you wore proudly on your back. The leather jacket, in particular, was the ultimate badge of cool, but other jackets like varsity jackets, denim jackets, and even the iconic bomber jacket also made their way into Poland. Each style brought with it a unique sense of identity. Wearing a denim jacket with patches or a bomber jacket in army green made you feel like you were living on the edge, stepping out of the expected mold.

The *varsity jacket* symbolized the American high school experience, a life we could only imagine from the movies. In Poland, wearing one was a little rebellious, a way to signal that you were different, that you didn't quite fit the mold of uniformity. It was a silent nod to a lifestyle of freedom, of school sports teams, of independence and adventure. *Denim jackets*, too, had their own aura. A bit rugged, a bit rebellious, they became a wardrobe staple for anyone who wanted to channel that effortlessly cool, laid-back American vibe.

And of course, the *leather jacket* was in a league of its own. It was, and still is, the ultimate symbol of cool. Wearing one was like putting on a suit of armor—it made you feel untouchable, unstoppable, like the rebels and rock stars who made leather jackets iconic. It was a way to tell the world that you valued freedom, that you weren't afraid to be yourself, and that you understood the allure of the American outlaw.

The Significance of Style in a World of Uniformity

In Poland, where much of life was about fitting in, these pieces—sneakers, leather jackets, denim jackets—were a chance to stand out, to express who you were in a way that went beyond words. They were symbols of freedom, individuality, and the influence of American culture on a generation eager to carve out its own identity. Each item of clothing was more than just fabric or leather—it was a small piece of the American Dream, a reminder that you could still find a way to be different, to embrace your unique style, even in a world that encouraged conformity.

American fashion brought a touch of rebellion to everyday life, a quiet but powerful way of saying, "I am my own person." It didn't just change the way we dressed—it changed the way we saw ourselves, opening up a world of possibilities, one sneaker, one jacket, one piece of individuality at a time.

Smuggling the Dream – The Risks and Rewards of Bringing Freedom Back to Poland

In a time when Western goods were scarce in Poland, American brands weren't just fashion—they were symbols of freedom, individuality, and everything the West represented. Getting your hands on a pair of Levi's, a Nike sweatshirt, or a leather jacket was no small feat. These items were treasures, bringing with them a sense of rebellion, self-expression, and connection to a world that felt out of reach. But behind every piece of American clothing, there was often a story—of friends, relatives, or strangers who risked a lot to smuggle these prized goods back to Poland.

The Smuggling Routes – From America to Poland

Smuggling Western goods into Poland was a complicated process, filled with challenges and danger. People would often rely on relatives who had emigrated to the United States or Western Europe, or on Polish workers who managed to travel abroad for temporary work assignments. These people became essential links in a chain of quiet resistance, risking heavy fines and trouble with customs officials to bring back items that symbolized freedom. Suitcases became secret vaults, filled with jeans, jackets, sneakers, and cassette tapes, each item carefully packed and hidden.

Every trip was a risk. Customs agents at the airport or border were always on the lookout for items that could "corrupt" the culture and influence of the East. To bring back anything Western was to defy the restrictions that aimed to keep Poland closed off from the outside world. Those who dared to smuggle had to be clever, strategic, and willing to face serious consequences. Some hid clothing between layers of personal items, while others wore multiple pairs of jeans or jackets to avoid detection. Each item that made it past customs was a small victory against a system that tried to limit access to the outside world.

The Power of Levi's, Sneakers, and Leather Jackets

Levi's jeans, in particular, were worth their weight in gold. A single pair of jeans, worn by a relative or friend, could be passed along to dozens of people in the community who just wanted to try them on, feel the fabric, and dream of owning a pair for themselves. Wearing Levi's was like wearing freedom on your legs—it was visible proof that you'd touched a part of the American dream. People would save up money for months or even years to afford these items on the black market, where prices were sky-high. To have Levi's or a Nike sweatshirt was to own a piece of something bigger, something hopeful, even if it was only a single piece of clothing.

Leather jackets were another highly coveted item, symbolizing rebellion and individuality. In a world where conformity was the norm, a leather jacket stood out like nothing else. It was a mark of toughness and defiance, worn proudly as if to say, "I am my own person." And for those lucky enough to wear Converse or Nike sneakers, the experience was exhilarating. In Poland, where most shoes were simple and utilitarian, American sneakers felt almost magical. They were colorful, bold, and completely different from anything you'd see on the streets. Each pair represented a tiny piece of American culture, an item that made you feel like you belonged to something bigger.

A Network of Trust and Quiet Rebellion

The smuggling of Western fashion created a network of trust among friends, family members, and even strangers. People would hear of a friend's cousin going abroad and would quickly send money, asking them to return with specific items—Levi's, Wrangler jeans, or perhaps a cassette tape of the latest rock album. The black market became a bustling hub, with people trading stories, sharing tips on how to get items past customs, and exchanging whatever little American goods they could acquire. It wasn't just about the clothes; it was about the experience of finding a way around the system, of quietly resisting the restrictions imposed on them.

This network was a lifeline to a world that felt unattainable, and every transaction was an act of defiance. People weren't just buying jeans; they were investing in a piece of hope, something tangible that brought them closer to the freedom and individuality they dreamed of. Wearing these items wasn't just beyond the limits of your surroundings.a fashion statement—it was a way to declare, without words, that you believed in something

The Legacy of Smuggled Dreams

Today, it might be hard to imagine the value that one pair of jeans or a leather jacket once held. But for those who lived through it, each item carried the weight of dreams. The thrill of touching American fabric, of feeling the heft of a leather jacket or the smoothness of Nike sneakers, was unforgettable. It was a taste of what could be, a promise that there was a world beyond the borders and barriers.

In a place where everything felt limited, smuggled American fashion gave people the chance to feel limitless, even if just for a moment. Each item was a symbol of connection, defiance, and the desire for something more. And in this way, smuggling wasn't just about clothing—it was about keeping the spirit of hope and freedom alive, one pair of Levi's at a time.

Consumerism and Technology – Gadgets of the West

If there was one thing that could light up the imagination of a kid growing up in Poland, it was the allure of Western technology and the abundance of American products. In a world where choice was limited, and goods were rationed or in short supply, the gadgets and brands coming out of the United States seemed like something from a different planet. American technology wasn't just about function—it represented a lifestyle, a gateway to freedom, individuality, and the thrilling idea of having options.

From the compact thrill of a Sony Walkman to the instant magic of a Polaroid camera, Western gadgets were as much about aspiration as they were about convenience. Each device brought a sense of possibility, a promise that the future could be within reach and in the palm of your hand. And then there was the consumer paradise of products like Coca-Cola and McDonald's, symbols of choice and abundance that felt almost mythical in a world where options were a luxury. American consumer culture offered something Poland didn't: the freedom to choose, the thrill of variety, and the chance to express yourself through what you owned.

And finally, as the digital age arrived, the world itself began to shrink, with American companies leading the way into the new frontier of the internet. Suddenly, the vast ocean separating Poland from America became less daunting, and the culture, technology, and excitement of the West were available in real-time. American technology not only changed the way we lived but also connected us, allowing a glimpse into a world that had once seemed untouchable.

Walkmans and Polaroid Cameras – American Tech as the Stuff of Dreams

In a world where technology was often functional and limited, American gadgets like the Walkman and Polaroid camera were like beacons of innovation and freedom. They weren't just devices; they were symbols of independence, creativity, and a lifestyle that felt worlds away from the everyday reality in Poland. These gadgets were something to aspire to own, not only because of what they could do but because of what they represented—a connection to the excitement, individuality, and cool factor of the West.

The Walkman – A Personal Soundtrack

When the Walkman first appeared, it was nothing short of revolutionary. Imagine being able to carry your music with you wherever you went—a luxury that was almost unimaginable in Poland at the time. The Walkman wasn't just a cassette player; it was freedom in your pocket. Suddenly, you could escape into your own world, tuning out the noise around you with your favorite songs. For the first time, music was private, personal, something that could go with you on walks, bus rides, and even quiet evenings alone.

Owning a Walkman was like joining a secret club. It was small, sleek, and incredibly cool. In Poland, where most people still relied on large, stationary cassette players, the idea of having music available anywhere, anytime, was mind-blowing. Those who were lucky enough to have one wore it proudly, the unmistakable orange headphones a sign that they were in on something big. Every song felt more meaningful, more profound, when it was experienced through the Walkman. It turned the everyday into something cinematic, like having a personal soundtrack to your life.

Polaroid Cameras – The Magic of Instant Moments

Then came the Polaroid camera, another icon of American ingenuity. In a time when photography involved waiting days, sometimes weeks, for film to be developed, the Polaroid was pure magic. With a single click and a few seconds of waiting, you could hold a memory in your hands, the photo developing right before your eyes. For someone in Poland, where access to a camera and film was already limited, the Polaroid seemed like a futuristic device, something almost too good to be true.

Polaroid photos weren't just pictures; they were experiences. Each snapshot was a moment frozen in time, instantly captured and immediately tangible. Friends and family would gather around, watching in amazement as the image slowly appeared on the small square of film. Owning a Polaroid meant you could capture your world—your friends, your family, the places you loved—and hold those memories in your hands. Every photo felt special, a one-of-a-kind keepsake that could be shared instantly, a far cry from the typical process of waiting, developing, and hoping the photos would turn out well.

The Aspirational Allure of American Tech

In Poland, both the Walkman and the Polaroid camera were more than just gadgets; they were items to dream about, aspire to, and, if you were lucky, cherish. American tech products like these were rare and valuable, often smuggled in by relatives or friends who had traveled abroad. Getting your hands on one felt like winning the lottery, and every detail—the feel of the Polaroid's click, the sound of the Walkman's cassette winding—was savored.

These devices made life feel bigger, more vibrant, as if you were participating in a piece of American culture every time you pressed play or snapped a picture. They were a glimpse into a world that seemed filled with boundless creativity and endless possibilities, where people could take their music, their memories, their entire lives with them, wherever they went. For a generation growing up in a world with few luxuries, the Walkman and Polaroid were symbols of hope, joy, and the power of technology to make life richer.

In a time when the world often felt limited, American tech products like the Walkman and Polaroid showed that there was always a way to make life more colorful, more personal, and more connected. They weren't just items; they were dreams made tangible, a taste of freedom, and a reminder that technology could open doors to new worlds, even from thousands of miles away.

The Desire for Choice – American Products as Beacons of Freedom

In a world with limited options and minimal variety, American brands like Coca-Cola and McDonald's were more than just products—they were symbols of abundance, freedom, and the power to choose. Growing up in Poland, where shelves were stocked with basic, standardized goods, the sight of these American icons was something magical. Each product offered a taste of the West, a small but powerful reminder that in other parts of the world, people had choices. And to us, choice itself was something precious, something worth admiring and longing for.

McDonald's – A Slice of the American Dream on Floriańska Street

When the first McDonald's opened in Kraków, it was a moment that felt monumental. It was 1992, and the restaurant opened on Floriańska Street, one of Kraków's most famous and historic streets, still just as iconic today. McDonald's brought with it the unmistakable allure of America: golden arches, brightly lit counters, and that irresistible scent of fries and burgers. I remember standing in line, my heart racing with excitement as I finally experienced what I'd only seen in movies or heard about in stories.

That first *Happy Meal* was nothing short of legendary. I still remember unwrapping my first hamburger and taking that first bite. The taste was unlike anything I'd had before—a perfect mix of flavors that felt indulgent, rich, and impossibly delicious. And those fries! Perfectly crispy, salty, and so much better than anything I'd tried before. And then, as if the experience couldn't get any better, I discovered the toy inside my Happy Meal—a bright, colorful, and brand-new toy that seemed like a piece of magic in my hands. For American kids, maybe this was just an everyday treat. But for me, it was an event so grand and memorable that I remember every detail to this day.

McDonald's became a place that was more than just fast food. It represented choice, abundance, and the thrill of experiencing something that felt like a small piece of the American dream right in the heart of Kraków. Every time I walked down Floriańska Street and saw those golden arches, it felt like a glimpse into a different world, one where life was filled with options, where people could indulge in things just because they wanted to. For us, McDonald's wasn't just a restaurant; it was a gateway to a life that felt freer, more exciting, and wonderfully new.

The Legend of Cherry Coke

Then there was *Cherry Coke*, a drink that somehow managed to encapsulate the novelty and excitement of American flavors in a single can. Cherry Coke wasn't just another soda; it was a statement. Unlike the basic beverages we were used to, Cherry Coke brought a unique twist—a sweet, slightly tangy flavor that felt exotic and indulgent. The can itself looked striking, with bold colors and a hint of sophistication that made it stand out from anything on Polish shelves.

I remember the first time I tried to convince my mom to buy me a can of Cherry Coke. She saw the word "cherry" on the label and, not knowing English, associated it with the labels on wines and other alcoholic drinks. She was convinced it was some kind of spiked soda and firmly refused to buy it for me. It took a lot of convincing, and some help from others who assured her it was just a regular soda, but eventually, I got my hands on a can. That first sip was unforgettable—sweet, unique, and nothing like the ordinary colas we were used to.

For a while, Cherry Coke became a beloved favorite, a rare but cherished treat that felt like a symbol of freedom and luxury. But then, mysteriously, it disappeared from the shelves, only to be replaced by a new, modern version that just doesn't capture the same magic as the original. And even today, I find myself hoping that one day, *Coca-Cola* will bring back the true original Cherry Coke. To the Coca-Cola executives who may never read this: please, bring back the original!

The Power of Choice – A Taste of the West

These products—McDonald's hamburgers, Coca-Cola, Cherry Coke—represented something much larger than their flavors. They were a taste of variety, of abundance, and of a lifestyle where options were endless and tastes were celebrated. In a country where choice was often limited to a few standard options, American brands stood out as symbols of possibility. Each time we enjoyed one of these treats, we felt a sense of freedom, a reminder that there was a world out there filled with things to discover, enjoy, and savor.

For Americans, these products might have been everyday items. But for us, they were small luxuries, each sip and each bite carrying with it the essence of the American spirit—a spirit that embraced choice, celebrated individuality, and showed that even the simplest things in life could be special. And to this day, when I see a can of Coke or walk past a McDonald's, I can't help but feel a small spark of that original excitement, that taste of freedom that American products brought to a world that was hungry for something more.

The Rise of the Internet – Connecting to the American Dream

The internet revolution brought about a transformation that felt as thrilling as it was profound. American companies like Google, Yahoo, AOL, and later Facebook and YouTube, didn't just create a new tool—they opened the world to us in ways that had once seemed impossible. Suddenly, the divide between East and West felt smaller, and with a few clicks, we could access American culture in real-time. For someone in Poland, the internet wasn't just technology; it was a gateway to explore, discover, and connect with a life that had only existed in movies or stories until that point.

The First Steps into the Internet Age

When the internet first became accessible in Poland, it was both incredibly exciting and incredibly expensive. Few people could afford it at home, so public internet access became the norm. "Internet cafes" began to pop up in cities across Poland, often set up in dimly lit basements where rows of computers were lined up, each with a glowing screen connected to the vast digital world. These cafes were like portals, bringing together groups of eager kids, teens, and adults who wanted a taste of the internet, even if it was just for an hour.

The cost of using the internet was no small thing. I remember it being around 5 PLN per hour, which was significant compared to the cost of everyday items—after all, a loaf of fresh bread was only about 1 PLN. For that price, you could get five loaves of bread, which provided real sustenance. But despite the high price, people still flocked to these cafes, pooling together whatever they could to buy time on the internet. Kids would sit shoulder-to-shoulder, exploring websites, watching videos, and chatting online, soaking up every second of this rare and valuable access to the digital world.

A Window to American Culture

With the internet, American culture was suddenly right there at our fingertips. Music videos, movie trailers, American news, and even the latest trends in fashion, slang, and sports could all be experienced as they were happening. No longer did we have to wait for TV broadcasts or smuggled media; instead, we had immediate access to whatever we wanted to learn about, watch, or listen to. The internet made it possible to stay updated on everything from the latest Hollywood blockbusters to the rise of new music genres, opening up a whole new way to interact with American culture in real time.

Social media and websites like Yahoo or AOL's chatrooms made it possible to communicate directly with people from other parts of the world. Suddenly, you could "meet" an American friend, exchange stories, or even practice English with a native speaker—all from a small internet cafe in a Polish basement. This was mind-blowing and exhilarating, a sense of connectedness that gave life to everything we had seen on TV or heard about from those who had traveled abroad.

The Digital Revolution – Bringing the World Closer

As internet access expanded and prices began to drop, more people were able to bring it into their homes, though this was still an investment for many families. Even then, the connection was slow, often relying on dial-up modems that tied up the phone line and made that unforgettable crackling sound whenever you tried to connect. But despite the slow speeds, the internet was a revelation, and the first taste of truly unlimited access to American culture was worth every waiting second.

American companies became the backbone of this experience, as platforms like Google allowed us to search for anything we could imagine, and YouTube let us watch everything from Hollywood trailers to music performances. This access changed how we viewed the world and transformed American culture from something distant and abstract into something personal and immediate. The internet became a bridge, allowing us to explore life in

America, follow trends, watch the latest sports events, and even celebrate holidays like Halloween and Thanksgiving with a real sense of what they meant to people on the other side of the globe.

A Revolution That Redefined Our World

For those of us in Poland, the internet didn't just make American culture accessible; it made it feel like part of our own lives. It redefined our sense of possibility, showing us that there was more to the world than our immediate surroundings and that our dreams, interests, and aspirations could be shared with people thousands of miles away. It allowed us to join a global community, where the American dream was only a click away.

Today, the internet is a part of daily life, but back then, each hour spent online felt precious, an invitation to explore a new reality and dream bigger than ever before. The digital revolution didn't just connect us to the West; it empowered us to live a little more freely, to break down barriers, and to feel, even in the smallest way, that we were part of something larger, something shared.

American Ideals – Freedom, Individualism, and Ambition

From movies to music, products to politics, America has always been about more than just its culture and innovations; it represents a set of ideals that resonate around the world. For many, especially those of us who grew up in countries where these values weren't always accessible, the American ideals of freedom, individualism, and ambition have been a powerful source of inspiration and hope. The vision of America wasn't just a place; it was a dream of self-determination, a belief that everyone has the potential to carve out their own path, make their own choices, and pursue success on their own terms.

In Poland, where collectivism and conformity were central to the way of life, these ideals felt refreshing, almost radical. The American notion of freedom—the ability to speak your mind, choose your own destiny, and chase after your dreams—stood in stark contrast to the limitations we often felt. American individualism celebrated the unique, the daring, and the independent, and for those of us living in a world that prized sameness, it was like discovering a new dimension of possibility. And ambition, the belief that with hard work and determination, you could "make it," became a defining trait of the American spirit that many of us admired and aspired to emulate.

Each of these ideals shaped the way we saw ourselves and the world, sparking dreams and ambitions that felt uniquely possible in the American vision of life. In the following sections, we'll explore how these values of freedom, ambition, and the pursuit of individual dreams became a lasting influence, reshaping our aspirations and inspiring a belief in the power to shape our own futures.

The American Dream in Your Mind – Freedom and Success as Aspirations

Growing up in Poland, the American Dream was more than just a phrase—it was an idea that represented everything we didn't have and everything we dreamed of achieving. The ideals of freedom and success, so deeply woven into the American spirit, became aspirations that shaped the way we saw ourselves and what we hoped to accomplish. The American Dream promised a life where you could overcome any obstacle, create your own path, and build a future defined by your passions and hard work. It was about more than material success; it was a philosophy of self-determination, resilience, and endless potential.

The concept of "freedom" as an essential part of success was something that seemed inherently American. For us, freedom wasn't just about physical or political liberty—it was a way to live without limits, to be able to pursue your dreams without anyone telling you it wasn't possible. American movies, books, and stories filled our minds with characters who weren't bound by their circumstances. People in America didn't wait for permission to dream—they took their futures into their own hands, confident that, with enough effort, they could succeed. This belief was transformative for those of us who grew up in a place where ambition was often tempered by limitations.

Success as a Personal Achievement

The American Dream also taught us that success was something personal, something that wasn't necessarily handed down but earned. It wasn't a collective goal or a measure of national achievement—it was about the individual. This sense of personal accomplishment made success feel like something uniquely attainable, something worth striving for. American success stories, like those of entrepreneurs who had started with nothing, artists who became stars, or athletes who rose to greatness, taught us that one's beginnings didn't determine one's future. This sense of personal achievement inspired a belief that each of us could, in our own ways, "make it."

In Poland, the collective mindset often emphasized the importance of fitting in and contributing to the whole rather than standing out. But the American Dream presented a different way of thinking, where success was deeply personal, measured by your own goals and values, not by society's expectations. It was a call to be ambitious, to chase dreams that might have felt impossible but, somehow, didn't seem so far out of reach. For me and many others, it created a spark—a quiet determination to aim higher, to explore what we could become, and to pursue goals that might have felt unrealistic if not for the inspiration of the American Dream.

Freedom and Ambition as Everyday Values

What made the American Dream so influential was that it wasn't just an abstract ideal. It was something woven into the everyday lives of Americans, from how they spoke to how they set goals and celebrated their successes. Freedom and ambition were everywhere, in the songs they listened to, the movies they made, and even the way they viewed failure—not as something to fear, but as a stepping stone toward eventual success. It made the pursuit of dreams feel exciting, worth the risk, and something to be celebrated.

This ideal of freedom encouraged us to take risks, to believe that our futures weren't limited by the place we came from or the systems we grew up in. It wasn't about achieving perfection; it was about having the courage to try, to go beyond the boundaries of what was expected or normal. In America, individuality was celebrated, and so was the right to pursue success in your own way, on your own terms. That idea planted a seed of possibility in my mind—a belief that with determination and vision, even someone from a small town in Poland could create a meaningful life.

A Lifelong Influence

The American Dream remains an enduring influence, a philosophy that still inspires me to this day. It isn't about chasing wealth or fame; it's about knowing that my life is my own to create, that I am free to pursue what I value, and that success, however I define it, is something within my reach. For someone who grew up in a world where dreams often felt like distant fantasies, the American Dream provided a map—a reminder that, with hard work, courage, and a little bit of faith, anything is possible.

The American Dream didn't just change my perspective—it gave me a blueprint for a life filled with meaning, growth, and a sense of purpose. It continues to drive me forward, shaping my values, fueling my ambitions, and reminding me of the power of freedom, individualism, and the endless pursuit of what's possible.

Ambition and Opportunity – The Promise of "Making It" in America

For those of us who grew up in Poland, America represented more than just a distant land—it was a place where ambition was encouraged, where anyone could "make it" if they worked hard enough. This idea of personal opportunity felt completely different from the collective mindset we knew under communism, where ambition was often seen as secondary to the needs of the group, and personal success was limited by the rules of the state. In America, success was a personal journey, something each individual could define and pursue on their own terms. That promise, the idea that success was attainable for everyone, felt like a dream that was close enough to imagine but difficult to fully grasp.

The American Mindset – A Celebration of Ambition

The American way of thinking elevated ambition to something to be celebrated. American stories were filled with characters who started with nothing and built their way up, entrepreneurs who took risks, and individuals who pursued their dreams against all odds. Movies, books, and even everyday conversations conveyed that ambition was not only acceptable but encouraged. You were supposed to dream big, take chances, and believe that success was within your reach. This mindset made America feel like a place where limitations were merely challenges to overcome, where the only true restriction was the limit of one's imagination and drive.

Growing up in a place where life was often dictated by practicalities and restrictions, this outlook was nothing short of inspiring. It made ambition feel like a form of courage, a daring expression of one's identity and dreams. In America, ambition wasn't seen as selfish or disruptive; it was considered an essential part of the individual journey—a way to contribute to society by pursuing what you were passionate about. This belief in individual potential, the drive to better oneself and make an impact, became something I deeply admired and aspired to embody.

The Collective Mindset of Communism – Limits on Individual Success

In Poland under communism, the idea of personal ambition was often overshadowed by the needs of the collective. The system prioritized uniformity and equality, aiming to ensure that everyone received the same basic standard of living, but often at the cost of personal achievement and growth. The emphasis was on contributing to the state, fulfilling a designated role, and not standing out too much. Individual success was often seen as secondary to the greater good, and personal aspirations could even be seen as a threat to the collective order.

Opportunities for growth and advancement were limited, and career paths were often predetermined by the state. The concept of "making it" in the way Americans understood it—as a unique, individual journey defined by personal choices and hard work—felt almost impossible. The state's control extended to education, employment, and even personal decisions, limiting the ability to truly pursue one's ambitions. Success was rarely about individual satisfaction; it was about fulfilling a role within a system that viewed ambition as something to be tempered and controlled.

In this environment, people were often taught to keep their heads down, to be cautious with their dreams, and to prioritize stability over personal growth. For many, ambition was a quiet, private matter, something that couldn't easily find expression. The freedom to choose one's path and to define success on personal terms was an idea that felt almost foreign.

The Appeal of American Opportunity

The contrast between these two mindsets made America feel like a place where dreams could truly be realized. In America, the "land of opportunity," people were encouraged to take risks, pursue their passions, and strive for success on their own terms. The concept of "making it" wasn't about fitting into a predefined role; it was about defining your own path, embracing your individuality, and aiming for the life you wanted. The freedom to choose one's destiny, to fail and try again, and to pursue a vision of success that was uniquely yours was a powerful idea.

In the American model, ambition wasn't a private hope—it was a public right, a way to contribute meaningfully to society while fulfilling one's potential. It made success feel like something anyone could attain, regardless of background, social status, or starting point. The stories of self-made individuals, people who built something from nothing, were the epitome of this mindset and made it clear that America was a place where, if you worked hard and dreamed big, you could achieve things that might have once seemed out of reach.

A Lasting Inspiration

The American ideals of ambition and opportunity remain a source of inspiration, a reminder that success doesn't have to be defined by external limitations or collective expectations. The idea that "making it" is a personal journey, one that values resilience, innovation, and self-belief, continues to influence the way I see the world. In a place like America, where ambition is encouraged and opportunity is celebrated, dreams can become realities. And that belief in personal potential has left a lasting mark, inspiring me to pursue my own ambitions with a sense of freedom and determination that I never would have known otherwise.

A Life of Choice – America's Promise of Freedom to Forge Your Own Path

For those of us who grew up in Poland, where choices were limited and many aspects of life felt predetermined, America represented the ultimate freedom—the freedom to choose your own path. In America, life seemed to be about options and the empowerment to make decisions that reflected who you were, not just what the state or society expected you to be. The idea of having control over your own life, of shaping your own destiny, was something that felt uniquely American, a promise that inspired dreams of individuality and independence.

Freedom to Choose – A New Way of Thinking

In the America we saw on television and in stories, people didn't just work to survive or fulfill a role; they pursued careers that reflected their interests, made lifestyle choices that matched their values, and defined success in deeply personal terms. Whether it was choosing a career, deciding where to live, or even expressing personal beliefs, Americans seemed to live by their own rules. The freedom to choose wasn't limited to monumental decisions, either—it extended to the small, everyday things that made life feel vibrant and meaningful. People could choose where to shop, which brands to wear, which books to read, and which causes to support.

In Poland, such choices often felt restricted. Options were dictated by availability, necessity, or even the government. The ability to shape one's own path was something most people could only imagine, as the focus was on collective stability rather than individual fulfillment. But in America, the idea of personal choice went beyond just options; it was a core value, a way of life that embraced the idea that each person should have the power to steer their own course, free from limitations. For someone who had grown up with limited options, this idea was powerful, revolutionary, and deeply inspiring.

The Impact of Individual Freedom

In America, individual freedom seemed woven into the very fabric of society. It was the reason people could take risks, follow unconventional paths, and be unafraid of standing out. This freedom allowed people to explore their passions, create their own identities, and define what happiness meant to them. It was a mindset that celebrated diversity, not just in culture but in thought, lifestyle, and ambition. For those of us on the outside looking in, this freedom was transformative—it represented a life where personal choice was not just allowed but celebrated as an essential part of existence.

American culture placed a high value on self-expression and autonomy. The country's icons, from rebellious rock stars to entrepreneurs and visionaries, all embodied the spirit of individuality and the belief that every person had a unique path to follow. Watching this from afar, the freedom to be yourself, to choose your own way forward, felt like an invitation to imagine a life where you weren't defined by circumstances or expectations but by your own desires and aspirations. It offered a sense of agency and empowerment that made life feel richer, more expansive.

The Right to Dream and Make Decisions

One of the most remarkable aspects of America's culture of choice was the idea that you had the right to dream big and make decisions that supported those dreams. In Poland, personal dreams often had to be tempered by practicalities, by the realities of a system that prioritized survival and stability over personal fulfillment. In America, however, people pursued their goals with a kind of boldness that was inspiring. The freedom to make mistakes, try new things, and take risks was not just a luxury; it was a given.

The right to choose your path meant that people could try different careers, move across the country, and even reinvent themselves. This freedom wasn't just about what you could have—it was about who you could become. It taught me that life didn't have to be a single, unchanging story but could be a dynamic journey shaped by choices. America symbolized the belief that life is about exploration, growth, and the power to follow your heart, no matter how unconventional or bold the journey might seem.

A Lasting Inspiration – The Freedom to Be Yourself

Today, the American spirit of choice and individuality continues to inspire me. It's a reminder that life can be what you make of it, that there's power in making your own decisions, and that you are free to pursue the life that aligns with your values and dreams. The idea that life is filled with possibilities, that there is no set path but only the one you create, has become a guiding principle. America's promise of choice isn't just an ideal; it's a way of thinking that encourages self-discovery and growth, inspiring me to embrace my own journey with a sense of curiosity and confidence.

In the end, America's symbol of freedom and choice is more than just a cultural ideal—it's an invitation to live fully, to trust in your own vision, and to believe in a future shaped by your own hands. It's a reminder that no matter where you start, life is a series of choices, and each one is an opportunity to step closer to the life you truly desire.

Conclusion – America in My Heart

As I look back on the many ways American culture has woven itself into my life, I'm reminded that the impact of a place goes far beyond its borders. Growing up in Poland, America was more than just a country across the ocean; it was an idea, a symbol of freedom, creativity, and the joy of living life on your own terms. Through its cars, motorcycles, music, movies, and TV shows, America became an influence, shaping my interests, my values, and even my sense of identity. In many ways, America has lived in my heart, a part of me that constantly inspires and reminds me of the endless possibilities in life.

Each of these cultural icons—whether it's the roar of a Harley, the beats of a rock anthem, or the thrill of an action film—has left an enduring mark. And yet, despite feeling connected to American culture in countless ways, there remains a dream that's as powerful as ever: the dream of one day experiencing these icons in person, of crossing that ocean to stand in the land that has inspired so much of who I am.

In the final reflections of this book, I'll explore how America's influence continues to shape my passions, how it fuels my dreams for the future, and why I believe that American pop culture holds a power beyond entertainment. It creates connections, transforms perspectives, and touches lives—even those that might seem far removed from the lights of Hollywood or the rumble of Route 66.

America's Enduring Influence – Shaping My Passions to This Day

Even now, decades after I first encountered the wonders of American culture, its influence remains as strong as ever. American cars, motorcycles, music, movies, and TV shows continue to shape my interests, fuel my passions, and fill my life with excitement and meaning. These cultural icons, which were once just glimpses of a distant dream, have become a permanent part of who I am. They're more than just hobbies or pastimes; they're elements of a lifestyle, a set of values, and a way of thinking that I carry with me every day.

Cars and Motorcycles – A Love That Only Grows Stronger

American cars and motorcycles were some of the earliest symbols of freedom and individuality that captivated me, and to this day, they hold a special place in my heart. Whether it's the sleek lines of a *Chevrolet Corvette*, the iconic curves of a *Ford Mustang*, or the raw power of a *Harley-Davidson*, American vehicles aren't just machines—they're symbols of personal expression and independence. Each time I see or hear one, I feel a rush of excitement that reminds me of the dream of owning one, the sense of freedom that comes with the open road.

My Moto Guzzi Breva 750, parked in my garage, is my own tribute to the American motorcycle spirit. And yet, the dream of owning a Harley-Davidson is still alive—a reminder of a lifelong aspiration sparked by the stories, images, and movies of my youth. I may not be in America, but every ride I take on my bike connects me to that spirit of adventure, and it's as if the roads I travel are my own little pieces of Route 66.

The Everlasting Power of Music

American music, too, continues to be a soundtrack to my life. From *Metallica* and *Nirvana* to *Green Day* and *The Offspring*, American bands bring a sense of intensity, passion, and raw emotion that makes every song feel like an anthem. The power chords of rock, the soulful melodies of blues, and the rebellious energy of punk all resonate deeply, filling me with a feeling that's both grounding and uplifting. These songs are more than just music—they're memories, moments, and motivations that stay with me, inspiring me to embrace life fully and live with purpose.

The impact of American music on my life goes beyond just the notes and lyrics; it's the way these songs have taught me to see the world, to channel emotions, and to find strength in times of challenge. And every time I attend a festival or a concert, it feels like I'm connecting to that American legacy, that spirit of music that has reached across oceans to touch lives like mine.

Movies and TV Shows – Stories That Still Inspire

American movies and TV shows are constant sources of inspiration, reminders of the dreams and ideals I grew up with. Whether I'm watching an action-packed *Fast and Furious* film or revisiting classic shows like *Knight Rider* and *The X-Files*, these stories continue to offer a sense of excitement and wonder. They're reminders that adventure, courage, and resilience aren't just themes in Hollywood—they're principles that can guide my own life.

These shows and movies don't just entertain me; they shape how I think, fuel my sense of adventure, and provide a sense of connection to the American ideals of freedom and possibility. Shows like *Breaking Bad* and *The Office* continue to remind me that success, struggle, and humor are universal. Each film and series I revisit feels like returning to a part of my own story, a way to reconnect with the dreams and aspirations that American culture instilled in me long ago.

A Lasting Influence Beyond Entertainment

American culture hasn't just been something to watch, listen to, or admire; it's been a way to learn, grow, and become who I am today. It taught me to dream big, to see the world as full of possibilities, and to value individuality and freedom. Even though I grew up far from the places and stories I admired, American culture became a bridge, connecting me to a world of ambition, passion, and creativity that I could aspire to.

Today, American cars, music, movies, and TV shows are more than just interests—they're reminders of a journey, of a dream that has stayed with me. They're a testament to the power of culture to shape perspectives, inspire aspirations, and create connections that cross boundaries. And as I continue to explore these passions, I know that a part of America will always be with me, guiding me, inspiring me, and reminding me that the dreams we hold close are never out of reach.

What the Future Holds – A Dream of Experiencing America in Person

As I look toward the future, the dream of finally visiting America remains one of my most cherished ambitions. The idea of experiencing in person the places, symbols, and cultural icons that have shaped so much of my life fills me with both excitement and a touch of caution. It's natural, I think, to worry about the "meet my hero" syndrome—that fear that, in reality, my dream might fall short of the America I've imagined. But despite these doubts, I hold onto the hope that America, with all its complexities and contradictions, will live up to the vision that has inspired me for so many years.

I dream of walking down iconic streets, seeing the glitz of Hollywood, the buzz of New York City, and the vast, open roads of the American countryside. I imagine myself experiencing the rumble of a Harley-Davidson as I ride along the legendary Route 66, soaking in the freedom and adventure that American culture celebrates. And as much as these places and experiences call to me, it's the people—the spirit of Americans—that I hope will truly make the journey complete.

I believe that despite its struggles, both internal and external, America remains a place where the ideals of freedom, individuality, and opportunity continue to thrive. I have faith that the American people, with their resilience, openness, and creativity, will welcome me into the heart of their country and make my journey as incredible as I have always imagined. For me, America has always been more than just a destination; it's a symbol of hope and possibility, a place where dreams are worth pursuing.

And so, while I may carry a small fear that reality might differ from my imagination, I trust that the spirit of America will live up to its reputation as my "hero"—a nation that, despite its challenges, remains a place of inspiration and endless possibilities.

The Power of Pop Culture – American Influence in the Most Unexpected Places

In the end, American pop culture is so much more than just entertainment. It's a force that transcends borders, languages, and generations, reaching into the most unexpected places and shaping lives in profound ways. Growing up in Poland, I never imagined how deeply the movies, music, cars, and ideals of a faraway country could impact my sense of identity, my values, and even my dreams. American culture has been a guide, a teacher, and a constant source of inspiration, sparking ambitions and instilling beliefs that I carry with me every day.

What makes American pop culture so powerful is that it speaks to universal human experiences—freedom, resilience, individuality, and the courage to pursue one's dreams. It reminds us that, no matter where we are, we have the power to shape our own lives, to imagine a world filled with possibilities, and to celebrate the unique journey each person undertakes. The characters in American films, the riffs of American rock bands, and the sleek designs of American cars are not just symbols; they are reflections of values that resonate deeply, inspiring us to see our own lives in new and exciting ways.

In many ways, American culture has been my bridge to a broader, bolder world. It's helped me to think beyond my surroundings, to dream bigger, and to believe that life can be lived fully, on one's own terms. Through its pop culture, America has shown that entertainment can be more than just a pastime—it can be a catalyst for self-discovery, a source of courage, and a reminder that no dream is too far-fetched.

This influence doesn't just stop at the border of the United States; it lives on in the hearts and minds of people across the world. It has an undeniable power, bringing out the best in us, encouraging us to live authentically, and reminding us that, no matter where we come from, we are free to aspire, to create, and to connect. In my own life, American pop culture has been an enduring hero, a constant companion, and a reminder that there's always a bit of adventure waiting—if only we have the courage to chase it.

Conclusion

As I finish writing this book, I feel an overwhelming sense of gratitude for everything American culture has given me. Despite the thousands of miles that separate us, America has had a profound impact on my life, my dreams, and my sense of identity. The symbols of freedom, individualism, and ambition that American pop culture embodies have reached far beyond the shores of the United States, resonating deeply with people like me, growing up in places that were often restricted and limited. For me, America was not just a distant land but a beacon of possibility, a place where dreams were achievable, where creativity was boundless, and where people were free to live life on their own terms.

From the hum of a Harley-Davidson to the rebellious chords of rock and punk, from the cinematic tales of courage and heroism to the simple joy of fast food and pop culture, America has shown the world what it means to live fully, to embrace life with open arms, and to celebrate the unique journey each person undertakes. These cultural treasures aren't just forms of entertainment—they are symbols of freedom, reflections of a society that values individual expression and the courage to pursue one's own path. This sense of freedom, individuality, and ambition is America's greatest export, touching lives in the most unexpected places and inspiring millions around the world.

Through the stories I've shared, I hope I've conveyed the awe and admiration I feel for your culture and the dreams it has inspired in me. America is a land of resilience, creativity, and endless potential—a place that has given the world so much, even when its own struggles have been visible. For someone like me, who has grown up influenced by American ideals from afar, these cultural gifts have been transformative. They remind me, and all of us, that life can be as vibrant and expansive as we dare to imagine.

I don't want to delve into American politics here; instead, I encourage you to do your own research, reflect on what truly matters to you, ask questions, and expect answers. Remember that your choices reach beyond your borders and affect lives around the world, even those who have never set foot in your beautiful country. It's not just about me or Poland; there are millions—perhaps billions—whose lives are touched by your culture and your example. So, choose in a way that makes your country <u>great again</u>. Choose in a way that <u>makes the whole world great again</u>!

Thank you!

www.ingramcontent.com/pod-product-compliance
Lightning Source LLC
Chambersburg PA
CBHW061507250726
48657CB00005B/1746